Online Schools

Online Schools

BY JENNY MACKAY

LUCENT BOOKS
A part of Gale, Cengage Learning

GALE
CENGAGE Learning·

Detroit • New York • San Francisco • New Haven, Conn • Waterville, Maine • London

LIBRARY OF CONGRESS CATALOGING-IN-PUBLICATION DATA

MacKay, Jenny, 1978-
  Online schools / by Jenny MacKay.
    pages cm. -- (Technology 360)
  Includes bibliographical references and index.
  ISBN 978-1-4205-0942-7 (hardcover)
  1. Computer-assisted instruction--Juvenile literature. 2. Internet in education--Juvenile literature. 3. Educational technology--Juvenile literature. I. Title.
  LB1028.5.M129 2013
  371.35'8--dc23
                                2013001732

Lucent Books
27500 Drake Rd
Farmington Hills MI 48331

ISBN-13: 978-1-4205-0942-7
ISBN-10: 1-4205-0942-X

Printed in the United States of America
1 2 3 4 5 6 7 17 16 15 14 13

CONTENTS

"As we go forward, I hope we're going to continue to use technology to make really big differences in how people live and work."
—Sergey Brin, co-founder of Google

The past few decades have seen some amazing advances in technology. Many of these changes have had a direct and measureable impact on the way people live, work, and play. Communication tools, such as cell phones, satellites, and the Internet, allow people to keep in constant contact across longer distances and from the most remote places. In fields related to medicine, existing technologies—digital imaging devices, robotics and lasers, for example—are being used to redefine surgical procedures and diagnostic techniques. As technology has become more complex, however, so have the related ethical, legal, and safety issues.

Psychologist B.F. Skinner once noted that "the real problem is not whether machines think but whether men do." Recent advances in technology have, in many cases, drastically changed the way people view the world around them. They can have a conversation with someone across the globe at lightening speed, access a huge universe of information with the click of a key, or become an avatar in a virtual world of their own making. While advances like these have been viewed as a great boon in some quarters, they have also opened the door to questions about whether or not the speed of technological advancement has come at an unspoken price. A closer examination of the evolution and use of these devices provides a deeper understanding of the social, cultural and ethical implications that they may hold for our future.

Technology 360 not only explores how evolving technologies work, but also examines the short- and long-term impact of their use on society as a whole. Each volume in Technology 360 focuses on a particular invention, device or family of similar devices, exploring how the device was developed; how it works; its impact on society; and possible future uses. Volumes also contain a timeline specific to each topic, a glossary of technical terms used in the text, and a subject index. Sidebars, photos and detailed illustrations, tables, charts and graphs help further illuminate the text.

Titles in this series emphasize inventions and devices familiar to most readers, such as robotics, digital cameras, iPods, and video games. Not only will users get an easy-to-understand, "nuts and bolts" overview of these inventions, they will also learn just how much these devices have evolved. For example, in 1973 a Motorola cell phone weighed about 2 pounds (.907kg) and cost $4000.00—today, cell phones weigh only a few ounces and are inexpensive enough for every member of the family to have one. Lasers—long a staple of the industrial world—have become highly effective surgical tools, capable of reshaping the cornea of the eye and cleaning clogged arteries. Early video games were played on large machines in arcades; now, many families play games on sophisticated home systems that allow for multiple players and cross-location networking.

IMPORTANT DATES

1728
Caleb Phillips offers the first distance learning class by mail.

1907
The human voice is transmitted electro-magnetically, giving rise to radio.

1929
Television is invented.

1953
The University of Houston offers televised courses.

1969
ARPANET, ancestor of the Internet, transmits a message from UCLA to Stanford University.

1700   1900   1920   1940   1980

1922
Penn State University offers class lectures by radio.

1876
Alexander Graham Bell invents the telephone.

1944
Mark I is built, the first programmable digital computer in the United States.

1973
The portable cellular telephone is invented.

in the Development of Online Schools

1997
Wireless Internet access (WiFi) is invented.

2010
The number of Internet-capable devices worldwide reaches 5 billion.

1989
University of Phoenix launches the world's first online college.

1999
Broadband Internet access provides the first high-speed method of getting online.

1985   1990   1995   2000   2005   2010

1995
Washington Internet Academy becomes the first online K–12 school option.

2003
The first 3G cellular phone network arrives in the United States.

1990
Tim Berners-Lee creates the World Wide Web.

1997
California Virtual University is established, offering seven hundred online courses.

2011
6 million college students and 250,000 K–12 students attend school online in the United States.

School's Virtual Facelift

In Texas, a fifth-grader turns on her computer at 10 A.M. and visits an online chatroom to say good morning to her teacher. In Idaho, a seventh-grader leaves his bedroom shortly before noon and heads down the hall to the kitchen to make a sandwich between his history and science classes. In California, a high school junior downloads an assignment from her chemistry teacher at 5 P.M., finishes it after dinner, and turns it in by uploading it at 9:30 P.M. All three students attend school every day, but they do not walk, ride a bike, or take a bus, and their school day does not always happen between the hours of 7 A.M. and 4 P.M. They are among the quarter of a million U.S. students in kindergarten through high school who attend school online, a population growing by about 25 percent every year. Among U.S. colleges, the online learning population is even bigger at more than 6 million students and is growing at five times the rate of new enrollments in traditional college courses.

Online education replaces traditional school buildings and classrooms with virtual ones. Today's students live in a world where people are doing more of their daily activities online, from communicating with friends and coworkers to shopping, managing their bank accounts, and dating. Traditional schools and classrooms, at least in the United

States, are still the places where a vast majority of students learn, but that could change in the future. Classroom-style learning from textbooks, surrounded by a teacher and peers who live nearby, may not keep pace forever with the increasingly Internet-ruled lifestyle of today's human population.

Already, traditional U.S. schools are seeing the value of teaching and learning in an online format. Many colleges and even some high schools now require students to take at least one online class before they graduate. Ignoring the potential advantages of online education could mean that the U.S. education system will begin to lag behind other developed nations whose students use online education more broadly.

Technology experts and inventors agree that the United States cannot afford to ignore online learning. Bill Gates, cofounder of the Microsoft Corporation, the world's largest software developer for personal computers, says people are

Computers and online tools have become increasingly important to education in recent years.

only beginning to realize the vast potential of online education. "So far technology has hardly changed formal education at all," he says. "But a lot of people, including me, think this is the next place where the Internet will surprise people in how it can improve things."[1] It is no longer a question of whether there *should* be online schools—they already exist and thrive. Educators instead face the question of how to best include online school formats in the lifestyles of today's learners.

CHAPTER 1

A History of Learning Outside the Classroom

The United States won its independence from England in 1776. Ever since then, Americans have believed in a strong system for educating all citizens, although they have not always agreed about the best way for that to happen. Public education in the United States has seen dramatic developments. The population has increased. People's lifestyles have changed. Perhaps most important of all, technological developments have transformed what students need to learn to get along in the modern world—and *how* they learn it. For many generations, formal education happened in a school building away from home, with a group of students learning from a teacher at the front of the room. In today's computer-centered world, the format of school itself is beginning to adapt. More and more U.S. schools and students, from kindergarten to college, are exploring the possibilities of online learning.

Distance Barriers to Learning

In the earliest years of U.S. public education, schools were often single-room buildings that served students of all ages and learning abilities. These students spent their school days in the same space and usually with only one teacher, typically an unmarried young woman. These one-room

Early American schools were often small, one-room structures, where students of all ages attended together. This historic schoolhouse in Ft. Lupton, Colorado, was built in 1875.

schoolhouses served the small, rural towns scattered across the nation. Teachers were usually compensated with a free place to live and meals from the people in town. In exchange, a teacher was mainly responsible for making sure students could read and do basic math—skills that were necessary for success in life.

Students usually spent about six to nine months of the year attending school. Many one-room schoolhouses were located in farming communities, and the school year was organized to leave summer months free for students to help their families with planting, tending, and harvesting crops. The colder months were reserved for school. In very cold climates, this created challenges for students who lived far from the schoolhouse. There were no cars or school buses, so getting to school required walking, riding a horse, or taking a wagon. In especially snowy or icy weather, this was difficult for some students and families to arrange. "In rural areas, students needed to travel long distances to school, which, given the transportation limitations of the day, was a major obstacle,"[2] says education professor William H. Jeynes. Parents of children from rural areas taught their school-age children at home when it was too difficult or time consuming to travel to school.

Higher education was an even bigger problem. Colleges and universities, which taught skills needed for professions in business, medicine, the arts, and other careers, were almost impossible for students to attend unless the students lived on or near the campus. As a result, those who lived in the most rural communities had the least access to higher education.

Mail-Order Education

Innovative teachers and professors looked for ways to make education more accessible for everyone, no matter where they lived. One obvious solution was to use the mail. In 1728, Caleb Phillips of Boston, Massachusetts, developed the first known distance-learning course for adults. Phillips taught a type of writing called shorthand and began offering instruction at a distance, using weekly mail-in lessons. He would mail the handwritten instructions to students, who would practice the exercises he assigned and mail back their lessons. According to Phillips's 1728 ad in the *Boston Gazette*, "Persons in the Country desirous to Learn this Art, may by having several Lessons sent weekly to them, be as perfectly instructed as those that live in Boston."[3]

Distance learning by mail, also known as correspondence learning, caught on throughout the United States. By the mid-1800s, improvements in the U.S. Postal Service made mail an efficient way to communicate. New railroads crisscrossed the nation, so that by 1870 mail could travel from one end of the United States to the other by train in a few days. This had taken weeks or months when mail carriers rode horses. For the first time, adult learners living almost anywhere in the country could take college courses by mail.

In 1882, the University of Chicago became the first U.S. university to create a home study division. It was now possible to earn a diploma or a college degree without moving to live near campus. The trend caught on, and other colleges and universities began providing distance education to meet the rising demand for classes completed by mail.

Education Spans the Continent

While trains increased the efficiency of the postal service, other technological advances in the late 1800s affected the possibilities of distance learning even further. By the 1850s, people were using an invention by a man named Samuel Morse. The new device, called a telegraph, sent surges of electricity along a wire stretched between two locations. This flow of electricity could be interrupted to create long

Cell Phones Go Digital

The world's first portable cellular telephone, the Motorola DynaTAC 8000X, was invented in 1973. It could store thirty phone numbers and had a battery life of about one hour. The DynaTAC used analog technology: signals (human voices) were passed in continuous streams over air waves. The phones were available to the public by the early 1980s for about $4,000 apiece. Not many people could afford one. Also, the phones were not especially portable at more than 1 ft (30cm) long and weighing 2 lb (1kg).

Cell phone lineage has now entered its fourth generation. Today's devices would be unrecognizable to the 1980s user. The 3G and 4G (third- and fourth-generation) phones are digital, transferring the human voice as bits of data rather than analog waves. They are pocket-sized, affordable, and most people own one. They store limitless contact numbers. They can snap and store photographs, hold digital music, search the web, send e-mails and text messages, play movies and TV, give directions to travelers, act as a personal secretary, and much more. They even transport students to virtual classes. These new, upgraded cell phones are indispensable devices that are becoming more useful with time.

and short pauses. Morse developed a code in which series of pauses of various lengths represented the different letters of the alphabet.

Telegraph operators could send brief messages across long distances using telegraphs and Morse code. A message could be sent and received almost instantly. The cost of telegraph messages, known as telegrams, was based on the number of letters and words used. They were therefore impractical for use in most distance-learning programs, but Morse's invention led to other technological developments that were a better fit for education at a distance.

Alexander Graham Bell was one inventor who expanded on Morse's idea of sending messages along an electrical wire. Bell created a way to send not just a coded jumble of starts and stops, but actual spoken words along a wire. His 1876 invention, at first called a speaking telegraph, soon

Alexander Graham Bell, the inventor of the telephone, inaugurates telephone service from New York, NY, to Chicago, IL, in 1882.

became known as the telephone. The technology was one of the most important inventions in U.S. history. It affected almost every citizen and industry and created new possibilities for distance education.

By the 1900s, students who received courses by mail could, in theory, speak to their instructors by telephone, ask questions, and have difficult concepts explained. Unfortunately, long-distance phone calls faced one drawback—the cost. "It could be argued that telephone teaching has not been used as much as it might have been in distance education because students were charged for using the service,"[4] says distance education consultant Tony Bates. However, the telephone was an important predecessor to later technology that did become widespread in distance education.

A Wave of Communication

One such invention that built on Bell's idea of transmitting sound over distances did so without relying on any wires to connect the speaker and listener. Guglielmo Marconi, an inventor from Italy, developed a way to use electromagnetic waves to conduct electricity across a distance. In 1899, Marconi sent a Morse code-style message across the English Channel from England to France without using wires. In 1901, he sent a similar message across the Atlantic Ocean.

Messages could now be transmitted through space without any wires at all. Ships at sea could communicate with each other using this wireless telegraph, something that had never before been possible. In 1907, another inventor, Lee de Forest, figured out how to use Marconi's invention to transmit the human voice. The earliest form of radio was born.

By 1915, U.S. inventors were exploring the vast possibilities of radio, which included broadcasting, or sending sound messages from one source along a particular electrical frequency in the air to any receiving device that was tuned into that frequency. News reports and music could be broadcast by radio to wide audiences. Events such as sports competitions and presidential elections could be reported over radio waves and brought into the homes of people who could not attend the event in person.

TECHNOLOGIES FOR DISTANCE LEARNING

Various technologies have been applied to the challenge of learning outside the traditional classroom setting. Each method has advantages and disadvantages.

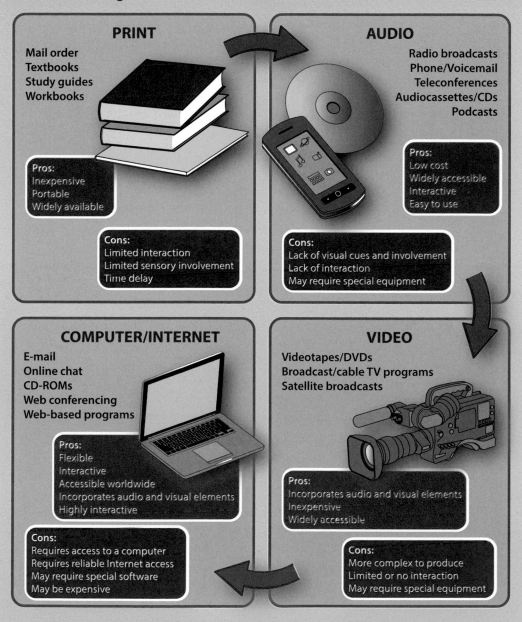

PRINT

Mail order
Textbooks
Study guides
Workbooks

Pros:
Inexpensive
Portable
Widely available

Cons:
Limited interaction
Limited sensory involvement
Time delay

AUDIO

Radio broadcasts
Phone/Voicemail
Teleconferences
Audiocassettes/CDs
Podcasts

Pros:
Low cost
Widely accessible
Interactive
Easy to use

Cons:
Lack of visual cues and involvement
Lack of interaction
May require special equipment

COMPUTER/INTERNET

E-mail
Online chat
CD-ROMs
Web conferencing
Web-based programs

Pros:
Flexible
Interactive
Accessible worldwide
Incorporates audio and visual elements
Highly interactive

Cons:
Requires access to a computer
Requires reliable Internet access
May require special software
May be expensive

VIDEO

Videotapes/DVDs
Broadcast/cable TV programs
Satellite broadcasts

Pros:
Incorporates audio and visual elements
Inexpensive
Widely accessible

Cons:
More complex to produce
Limited or no interaction
May require special equipment

By the 1920s, radios were part of the American lifestyle. Pennsylvania State University was the first to recognize that radio could also be used to teach students who were unable to attend classes in person. Some of the university's professors began offering distance courses by radio in the 1920s. "Educational institutions were excited about the idea of offering information to their students over airwaves and were eager to implement radio in the classroom,"[5] say online instructors Kent Farnsworth and Teresa Brawner Bevis. By World War II in the 1940s, more than two hundred colleges and universities in the United States had licenses to conduct some of their courses at a distance, using a combination of mail-in materials and lectures broadcast by radio.

Long-Distance Imagery

By the mid-twentieth century, most people received their news and entertainment through the radio and communicated with each other by telephone. In effect, technology was shrinking distances. People who lived nowhere near each other could have live conversations, and people who lived long distances from events such as baseball games, concerts, or university lectures could listen on their radios. Although these were ingenious ways of transmitting sound along wires and through the air, inventors were not satisfied with stopping at sound. They imagined a world where pictures could be sent along the same pathways, something that might revolutionize the sharing of news, entertainment, and education. Inventors around the world worked to find a way to add long-distance imagery—television—to long-distance sound.

An American named Philo Farnsworth was among them. Farnsworth was born in Utah in 1906 and spent his early childhood in a home with no electricity. When his family moved to Idaho, he discovered a collection of science magazines in the attic of their new home and was fascinated. When he was fourteen, Farnsworth showed a high school teacher his ideas for an invention he called an image dissector that would break camera images into small pieces and transmit them electronically. In 1929, Farnsworth created an all-electric camera eye tube that could record a still image and use electricity to transmit it onto another surface.

Farnsworth's device, when paired with Marconi's work on the transmission of electric signals through space using radio waves, made it possible not only to hear a person talking, but to see that person on the glass screen of a box that received the electronic signals and transmitted them into a picture. During a television broadcast, an image was broken down into tiny parts, or dots, each sent through the air as an electronic signal. Televisions tuned into the right broadcast frequency were able to receive the signal through a wire antenna. The television sets then reassembled the dots in the right order and displayed them on the glass television screen. People watching TV were able to see not just dots,

A New York City family watches television in the 1950s. After World War II, TVs became a staple of U.S. households, ushering in a new era of communication and entertainment.

but recognizable, moving images. The new device seemed to have limitless applications, including the ability to teach visually across long distances.

In the years after World War II, television sets were among the most popular new devices in the country. By 1960, 85 percent of U.S. households had a TV. Educators took great interest in television's potential for teaching and learning. Once televisions became common household devices, teaching experts began to recognize that television had the potential to follow in the footsteps of radio as a source of delivering lectures to students long distance. "The period from the mid-1950s to the mid-1960s can be labeled 'the decade of educational television,'"[6] say psychologist Robert A. Wisher and educational consultant Christina K. Curnow. Studies showed that students in traditional classrooms learned just as well from television broadcasts as from listening to a live, face-to-face instructor. Television seemed positioned to become a major new way for students to learn. "It (television) promised to reach farther than films with an aim of a television, *ergo* a classroom, in every home someday,"[7] say Wisher and Curnow.

Despite their seeming promise as a tool for distance learning, TV broadcasts never achieved the same status as the radio lectures delivered by hundreds of college professors in the 1920s and 1930s. Televisions were used in classrooms to supplement in-person lectures, but at home, Americans used television technology more for recreation than a way to obtain formal school lessons from a teacher long distance. Decades passed, and television and education remained mostly separate. Eventually, however, television technology became central to another new device that would truly revolutionize distance learning—the computer.

Computing Machines

Just as inventors dreamed of finding ways to communicate with other people across long distances, they also imagined machines that could automatically complete repetitive mental tasks like adding and subtracting, which were once considered core skills for students learning mathematics in schools. The Industrial Revolution, which began in Great Britain and spread around the world, was a period from about 1750 to 1900 in which machines and factories were invented to perform tiresome, repetitive, or dangerous physical tasks more efficiently. Such machines forged a path to the invention of the first computers, devices originally developed to perform repetitive math calculations automatically. Among its many benefits to businessmen, scientists, and other professionals, this technology would also make it easier for teachers and students to concentrate on learning higher-level math concepts necessary in a technologically developing world.

One early version of a modern computer was built in 1944 by inventors at Harvard University and a company called International Business Machines, known today as IBM. Called the Mark I, the machine was the first programmable digital computer ever made in the United States. It solved math problems using mechanical parts including levers, switches, and a 50-foot (15m) rotating shaft powered by an electric motor. Mark I was basically an enormous calculator. At 8 ft (2.4m) tall and 51 ft (15.5m) long, it weighed 5 tons (about 4,500kg). It was very inefficient, by modern standards, requiring four seconds to multiply numbers with numerous digits and ten seconds to divide them. Furthermore, it had only enough memory to store seventy-two numbers at a time.

Despite its limits, the Mark I was an important step in the beginning of the computer era that rapidly changed the way people communicated and learned. "Many important figures in the developing world of computers were introduced to the subject on the Harvard Mark I,"[8] says computer history professor Bernard Cohen. Using the same binary code system as Mark I, in which computer programs and directions are written and interpreted using combinations of just two digits, 1 and 0, computers soon became smaller, cheaper to build, easier to use, and capable of performing tremendous computational feats. The average computer used in homes and classrooms today can perform a billion mathematical computations per second and store billions of numbers in memory.

As computer technology became more advanced, scientists began to pair it with other twentieth-century technology, such as telephones, televisions, and radio waves. Computer designers combined these concepts into single machines that used television sets as monitors and telephone and radio technology for communication. Computers put some of the most significant discoveries of mankind to use in a single device at one time. They revolutionized entire industries, including education.

Computers Begin to Network

Though television never became the long-distance teaching tool that many scientists predicted, computers were another matter. In the 1960s, standalone computers were overtaken by computers that could be linked to communicate with each other. Calculations performed on one computer could be seen by other computers in the network. Data and information could be sent from computer to computer using some of the same communication technology that allowed telephones to transmit voices and televisions to transmit voices and images. The ability for computer users to easily share information, sound, and images made it possible for educators in one place to teach learners in another almost as efficiently as if they were in the same room. Whereas televisions allowed only one-way information exchange, linked computers allowed back-and-forth correspondence that vastly improved the experience of distance learning.

The first long-distance networked computer system was the ARPANET, which transmitted its first successful message from the University of California, Los Angeles to Stanford University in 1969. Four host computers were connected in different locations via ARPANET, and they were able to exchange various kinds of data. By the 1970s, scientists working on ARPANET had created applications, or ways of applying the new computer network technology. One such application was electronic mail, known as e-mail, in which a message could be sent from one host computer over the network to a designated receiving computer. Eventually ARPANET expanded to become the Internet, a vast system that can be accessed by any computer user in the world to communicate and exchange information with other computer users.

Throughout the 1960s and 1970s, Internet technology improved, and more users became familiar with its potential. At first, most of these users were working in fields such as national defense. In the 1980s, computers were still large, boxy contraptions that took up a lot of space. Businesses, schools, and private citizens had computers to perform tasks like typing and playing games, but most people did not yet consider the computer an essential tool for daily life. That changed with the Internet. Computers rapidly became more commonplace as the benefits of applications

Medical specialists and nurses work in an early computer room with an IBM computer in 1980. As computers evolved and became smaller in size, more and more businesses and people began to use them.

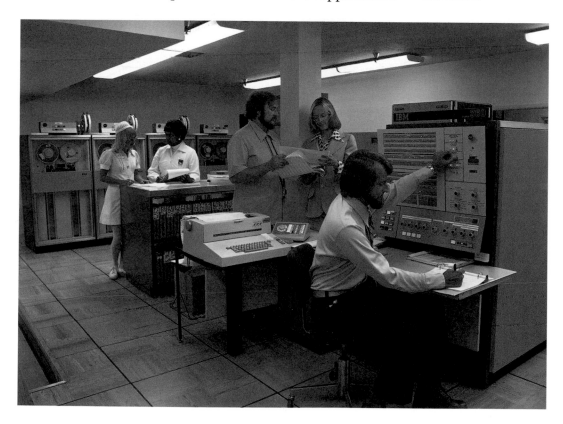

Famous Non-Traditional Students

Distance alternatives to the traditional classroom have always attracted successful, motivated, busy individuals. Charles Schulz, creator of the *Peanuts* comic strip featuring Snoopy and Charlie Brown, took only one formal art course, and it was through distance learning. Franklin D. Roosevelt, the thirty-second president of the United States, took distance courses before attending Harvard University and starting his political career. Arnold Schwarzenegger, actor and two-term governor of California, earned his college degree through distance learning, as did filmmaker Steven Spielberg. Professional basketball star Shaquille O'Neal earned his master's degree in business administration through an online school.

It is becoming more common for elementary, middle, and high schools to be offered online as well, serving students such as thirteen-year-old Jordan Windle of Indiana, the youngest diver to make the 2012 U.S. Olympic Team Trials, and Thia Megia, who in tenth grade was a finalist for the 2011 *American Idol* singing competition. Distance education, especially through online schools, is an increasingly popular option for students whose lifestyle makes it difficult to attend traditional schools.

Actor and politician Arnold Schwarzenegger used distance learning to earn his college degree.

like e-mail became more widely recognized. People realized that anyone could be part of the wide-reaching network of computer users, and they wanted to be included too. More people began using computers with Internet technology to communicate and learn.

Educating Through the World Wide Web

By the 1990s, computers had become a mainstay in the lives of millions of Americans. The Internet was a tremendous advancement in computer technology, but what really made computers indispensable was the World Wide Web. In 1990, computer scientist Tim Berners-Lee created an information-sharing system in which any computer user could create a website to store information at a specific digital address on the Internet. Computer users with Internet access and the website address could then access the same information by downloading, or transferring it, onto their own computers.

In the mid-1990s, the World Wide Web became available to users everywhere. Anyone with a computer could learn about almost anything over the Internet. A popular new pastime was "surfing the web," or exploring and investigating the web's vast and growing resources and abilities. People posted web content. People read web content. Suddenly, people could do almost anything online, from shopping to finding a date.

The World Wide Web began weaving various strands of learning possibilities into a fabric that educational professionals could hardly have imagined in previous years. Classroom teachers began using websites to teach students about exotic places, rare animals, historic events, and current news. Educators also saw that, finally, the traditional barriers to correspondence courses by mail and the inconvenience of learning through radio or televised lectures had vanished. With the World Wide Web, classes could take place completely online. A school needed only a website to which teachers could upload, or post, content. Students needed only to access that website to download spoken lectures, videos, and written lessons and to upload their own work. Teachers could instantly communicate with students using e-mail.

BITS & BYTES

5 billion

Number of Internet-connected devices in the world in 2010 (by 2020, there will be 20 billion).

In the same way that technology such as the telephone, television, and radio shrunk the world earlier, the World Wide Web was shrinking distances between schools, teachers, and students. Computers and the Internet made school possible from anywhere teachers and students could access a computer. "The Internet offers the means to deliver courses to new and different audiences who may be dispersed geographically and who may not have had the opportunity to study in a conventional setting,"[9] say education technology experts Steve Ryan, Howard Freeman, Bernard Scott, and Daxa Patel. Technology once again closed gaps, this time between teachers and learners.

Pioneers in Online Education

The University of Phoenix was one learning institution that immediately leaped onto the World Wide Web to teach students. Founded in 1976, the university's goal was to make college education accessible to working adults who could not attend a traditional college's typical lineup of daytime classes. By offering options such as evening and weekend classes, as well as distance-learning classes through the mail, the University of Phoenix had a history of helping college students learn in nontraditional ways. In 1989, it seized the opportunity to offer online classes and opened its first online campus, conducting degree programs completely through computer technology and the Internet. In 1991, the school granted degrees to its first group of students who had completed their college coursework entirely online.

The University of Phoenix was a pioneer in full degree programs that could be completed at a distance. Throughout the 1990s, other institutions of higher learning in the United States and Europe experimented with online education by offering certain courses and portions of courses online. The World Wide Web also brought changes to the kindergarten-through-twelfth-grade (K–12) school system. Students and parents in primary and secondary schools were previously limited to three basic options for school—attend a public school, attend a private school, or pull out of the school system altogether and homeschool.

In 1995, the state of Washington's Internet Academy offered a new choice to K–12 students—attend school online, much the way that college and university students were now able to do. The Internet had spawned an educational revolution.

Classroom Access Goes Digital

Computers and the Internet meant that physical distance was no longer a barrier to worldwide communication, idea sharing, and learning. Schools were no longer tied to so-called "brick-and-mortar" physical buildings as they had been since the days of one-room schoolhouses. Schooling could take place in the virtual world of the Internet; schools such as the University of Phoenix had proven this was possible.

A student walks into the main building of the University of Phoenix, in Phoenix, Arizona. In 1989, the university became one of the first institutions to offer education fully online.

Online Programs Can Handle Massive Class Sizes

Class size is one aspect of online learning that can be seen as both an advantage and a disadvantage. While class size in a traditional class is limited by the size of the physical classroom, online classes have no such limitations. On the other hand, having too many students in a class, whether online or face-to-face, leads to less teacher involvement with students.

Massive open online courses, or MOOCs, are a new and growing trend in online learning, and they underscore such concerns. Some colleges and universities now open MOOCs to everyone, regardless of age, location, or whether they are students of the college. Tens of thousands of students sometimes take a MOOC. They learn online and test their knowledge with interactive quizzes and activities. Offering such courses for credit is tricky. MOOC students have little to no personal contact with an instructor, and there is concern that cheating would be difficult or impossible to prevent. But MOOCs do offer educational opportunities to more curious people than ever before. They are just one of the new possibilities in online education.

However, in the early days of online education, students and teachers faced some challenges that still needed to be resolved. One was the slow speed of Internet access. Computers in the early days connected to the Internet with a dial-up connection, using technology that was similar to making a telephone call. Computers and the web exchanged data by sending analog signals—continuous waves of data—through phone wires, similar to the way phones send sound. The process was slow, interruptions and stalls were frequent, and people were not able to use a dial-up Internet connection and their phone at the same time.

Broadband Internet access, developed in 1999, helped overcome these obstacles. A broadband connection bypasses the traditional dial-up method of Internet access in one of two ways. It either sends and receives messages along an entirely different group of wires than phone wires (in a cable Internet connection) or it uses the same cluster of wires as the phone service but diverts Internet data along different individual wires using a piece of equipment called a micro-filter, which separates the wires used for telephone signals from those used by broadband Internet (this is the process used in digital subscriber line, or DSL, connections).

All broadband connections, whether cable or DSL, transmit text, images, and sound digitally. Bits of data are encoded as a combination or pattern of the digits 1 and 0. These digital bits pass through wires faster and more smoothly than analog data. Transferring digital data over a broadband connection happens almost instantaneously and without tying up a phone line in the process. Broadband is now a common method for accessing the Internet, allowing people to avoid the glitches of the dial-up system. Online students with broadband Internet access can view photos, videos, and other content online immediately and can even talk with their teacher over the phone at the same time.

Severing the Wires

Although broadband Internet access has vastly improved the ease and accessibility of learning online, the more recent advent of wireless technology has had even more of an impact on online education. Online schools once confined students to desktop computers at home, but wireless technology makes school as portable as the Internet. Students can access their lessons or talk to their teachers from anywhere. "Today courses are not just available in correspondence mode but also via real-time web conferencing tools, radio, CDs and DVDs, television, online chat, mobile phones, and many forms of technology-enabled learning environments,"[10] says distance-learning researcher Curt Bonk.

Wireless connections use some of the same concepts as radios and early television to transmit data to and from

A young woman uses her laptop on the steps of a building in Cadiz, Spain. Wireless Internet technology has given people the freedom to access the World Wide Web almost anywhere without the use of cords or cables.

a computer over air waves without depending on wires. People can now use a wireless Internet setup to surf the web from any room in their home or from any place that has a device for sending and receiving data wirelessly. Modern cell phones even allow people to access the Internet from hand-held devices, sending data over air waves much like television broadcast towers have done for a long time. Computers have taken the shape of portable, battery-operated laptops, handheld tablets, and phones, and they are everywhere.

Online education blends many of the best technological inventions of the past century to give schools a new shape and a new format. Physical distance between students and teachers is no longer a barrier to learning. As online school options grow in popularity, they are changing the way the world approaches education.

CHAPTER **2**

The Technology of Online Education

At any time of day, on any day of the year, almost anywhere in the United States, school can be in session. Teaching and learning have migrated outside the walls of brick-and-mortar school classrooms and beyond the traditional school day and school year. Learning now takes place underground and through the air, using technology to connect teachers and learners. The explosion of computer and online technology during the past three decades has transformed the daily lives of people all over the world, but perhaps for no one more than students. School used to mean a building full of classrooms, the classrooms full of students, with one teacher standing at the front of every room. This is still the way it is for the majority of the students, but every year, thousands more students are no longer pursuing their education in a classroom, but through a computer connection.

Online teaching and learning occur in a completely computerized world. Traditional brick-and-mortar schools are built with learning needs in mind. So are online schools. They have real teachers. They have real students. The teachers and students interact with each other. The interactions just happen to take place within the intangible Internet world known as cyberspace. "The technology allows us to have the essence of what we do in the classroom," says

Oceans Apart

The Internet links computers worldwide. Users on land are connected by a network of mostly underground wires, but 71 percent of Earth is covered by oceans. Many people have misconceptions about how Internet communication crosses these massive bodies of water. Satellites are often assumed to be the carriers, much the way broadcasts are transmitted to millions of television sets. However, the Internet crosses oceans by cable, not by satellite. Cables are deposited along the ocean floor to connect continents and allow the passage of information. They can carry much more data, and more quickly and reliably, than satellites can, making them a better option for ocean-spanning Internet use. Special ships lay the cable and can carry 1,243 miles (2,000km) of it at a time. The ships use a plough to dig into the ocean floor and bury heavy-duty cable designed to withstand high pressure and salt water. A cable ship can lay about 93 to 124 miles (150 to 200km) of cable per day. Placing cable on the ocean floor is tedious, difficult, and time-consuming, but the convenience of global communication and learning make it a worthwhile undertaking.

Daniel Perales, distance education coordinator for the University of South Florida. "Students don't feel so alone."[11]

Instead of spending money on chalkboards, desks, and chairs, online school designers spend money on the technology that links teachers and students in an online space. In online education, school is less of a place and more of an event. As technology evolves, online schools are increasing their capabilities and possibilities as fast as software developers can develop them.

Building Schools on a Network

Online schools, just like traditional schools, are centers of communication where teachers and students come together to share information—the information is just passed along in a different way. In an online school, communication relies not just on the spoken language of teachers and students, but also on the language of computers, which communicate via the Internet.

Communication, not education, was the original intention of the Internet, but education has benefitted greatly because of it. Just as the first telephones were based on a network of wires connected to endpoints—individual phones, each of which had a unique number assigned to it—the Internet is based on a network of wires. But the endpoints of the Internet are computers. Every computer with an Internet connection is linked to wires (or in the case of wireless connections, to a modem that is wired).

These wires all link to other wires that connect to nearby computers. Internet-linked computers in the same area are grouped together. The wires from this group are, in turn, connected to more wires connecting other groups of computers to form a still larger group. Bigger and bigger groups are connected by more wires. Eventually, they establish an enormous network with millions of computers, each able to communicate with any other computer that is also connected to the network, no matter where it is in the world. Teachers and students all around the globe use the Internet to share knowledge and enhance their learning experience.

Schools Without Walls

The ability of the Internet to link computer users together regardless of where they are frees students and teachers from the confines of any particular room or location. In the early days, computers could only access the Internet using a modem (short for modulator-demodulator), a device that converts data into a form that can travel over television or

Ethernet cables connect computers to the Internet via a network router. The Internet is primarily an enormous network of interconnected wires.

cable lines. The modem was connected to the Internet by wires, and the computer had to be connected to the modem by wires as well. Therefore, anyone who wanted to use the Internet had to work at a computer that stayed in one place because it was wired to an outlet in a nearby wall. Most early online learning, therefore, required a student to sit at the same desk, in the same room, to complete every lesson.

Wireless Internet technology has freed Internet users from stationary computers. Many modern modems take the form of a wireless router, a device that is attached to a wall (and the Internet) with wires but receives information from a computer using radio signals. Modern computers can convert data into a radio signal. Using an antenna, they send the information to the wireless router, which in turn, sends the data onto the Internet through wires. The process works in reverse to send information from the Internet back to the receiving computer.

As long as a computer with wireless technology is within range of a wireless router that it can access, the Internet is available. Computers have changed shape to take advantage of this new technology. Traditional desktop computers are now joined by portable laptops; they can be moved around a house, a yard, or an apartment building and still access the Internet. This makes online school portable and gives students more opportunities to engage in the world outside of a traditional classroom. "Technology will be used to create learning communities among students in new ways," says dean of Arizona State University's Online and Extended Campus program Philip R. Regier. "People are correct when they say online education will take things out of the classroom. But they are wrong, I think, when they assume it will make learning an independent, personal activity."[12]

One reason online learning does not trap students into solitary locations is that many public and social places offer wireless technology (called WiFi, short for wireless high fidelity), providing routers that support multiple devices all using the Internet at once. A WiFi "hotspot" is any place where a wireless router allows connection to the Internet. Hotspots are commonly found in places such as libraries, bookstores, restaurants, coffee shops, hotels, and public parks. Students, or groups of students, who take classes in online schools can therefore attend class wherever the Internet can be accessed by WiFi, potentially even meeting their peers in such places to do online projects together from their computers.

Online school is no longer bound by the walls of one room and the wires behind one desk. "The greater level of accessibility to course content and materials from nearly any location will encourage students to realize learning happens everywhere and at anytime, and is not confined to the classroom,"[13] says Jacey Waterhouse, a teacher at an online charter school in Hawaii.

School in a Cell

Wireless Internet technology has greatly expanded the options of online students who do not want to be tied down to one location while taking courses and exchanging information online. However, the options for Internet users continue to increase rapidly. No longer must online students and teachers rely on computers alone to access information and send and receive data. Modern cell phones now combine the best of telephones, radios, and televisions, making school more portable still.

Unlike wired telephones, often called land lines because they are connected to one another by land-based wires, cell phones use radio frequencies, operating much like radio stations. "First, of course, a cellphone is a telephone," says electrical engineer Guy Klemens, "but it is also a radio receiver and a transmitter, calling for an understanding of radio waves, antennas, and a history of radio."[14]

A cell phone has a built-in antenna that communicates with a transmission tower. During a call, the cell phone records the user's voice with a microphone and encodes the sound information into small bits of data that it transmits as a radio signal. The phone uses its built-in antenna to send the encoded information to the nearest tower. The tower sends out the encoded information to the receiving cell phone device, which uses *its* antenna and decoding abilities

A structure with cell phone, radio, and microwave devices towers over a state park in Los Angeles, California. Such towers are needed throughout the world for cellular technology, including 3G and 4G, to work.

to turn the information back into the sound of a human voice, transmitted through a tiny speaker.

The entire process happens in seconds. It works similar to the way citizens band (CB) radios have long worked for police officers, truck drivers, and others, but with important differences. For one thing, CB radios were one-way—only one person could talk at a time, and the listener had to wait until that person finished before beginning to speak. CB radios also had few frequencies, perhaps twenty-five in one area, and anyone with a radio tuned into that frequency could hear everything being said. Cell phones, on the other hand, use two-way communication, and a different frequency is assigned to each phone conversation, which makes them private and secure.

Cell phones also encode voice data digitally, using a computer's binary language of the digits 1 and 0. "Digital compression is used to shrink the streams of digits and save network capacity," say telecommunication experts Joseph Straubhaar, Robert LaRose, and Lucinda Davenport. "Digital transmission techniques make it possible for several users to share each channel."[15] Every cell tower hosts hundreds of frequencies, and each is able to support multiple users because of compressed digital data. This allows a tower to coordinate many private conversations at once. All of this is important for online students because, with cell phone technology, teachers can receive phone calls from students and answer questions at anytime, not just when they are on the computer.

Because so many people use cell phones, cities and towns need multiple cell phone towers to manage all the different frequencies and conversations. In fact, cities are separated into cells, small areas of a few square miles, and each cell has a dedicated tower for controlling the radio-wave conversations of cell phone users nearby. These different city cells are what give cell phones their name. A cell phone's antenna constantly scans to make contact with the nearest tower, so that if a user is in a moving car, the cell tower picking up the signal may change but the conversation is not interrupted.

Probably the biggest advantage of this traveling cell phone technology for online learning is that spoken conversations are not the only kind of information cell phones can process digitally. Many phones, called 3G and 4G devices (short for the third and fourth generations of cell phone technology), now also send and receive data from towers, which have wires connected to the Internet. As long as 3G and 4G phone users are in range of a cell phone tower, they can visit websites, send e-mail, download and upload songs and videos, and more. Students in online schools, therefore, no longer need to find a WiFi hotspot—their phone locates the nearest cell tower in range and can use it to access lessons, classmates, and their teacher online.

Smartphones can access the web with results as good as, if not better than, computer users with a WiFi connection. "3G networks boast broadband transmission speeds of 1–3 million bits per second, enough to send full-color pictures through your cell phone, to download your favorite music and video files, and to effortlessly surf the web on handheld computers,"[16] say Straubhaar, LaRose, and Davenport. Most phones with data abilities can readily access the websites and modern learning technology of online schools. Although the phones have limits (they do not, for example, make it easy for the user to compose and upload a typed term paper), they put school access at the fingertips of students on the go.

The Language of the Internet

Whether online students and teachers access school by computers physically wired to the Internet or ones that use wireless routers or cell technology, the foundation of the school experience is the hardware, or the physical objects that make up the computer or cell phone system. The hardware is what ultimately links the various endpoints, or terminals, connected by the Internet network. However, the Internet also requires something that is not physical—protocol, a computer-specific language that sends rules along the wires to specific machines to tell them what tasks to complete and how to complete them. All devices that connect to the Internet—including cell phones and tablets—must speak the same language, or protocol, in order to communicate. Just as teachers and students communicate by speaking the same language, computers connected to the Internet need a common language to communicate with each other.

Without a common language, any two computers that wanted to share information would have to have their *own* unique language, like a secret code known only to them.

This would be limiting for an online classroom—the teacher's computer would have to have a specific, shared language with the computer of every student in the class. A protocol, however, allows any two computers to share information. Of course, without a network of wires linking them all together, computers would not be able to "speak" to each other, even with the shared protocol. The Internet, then, works because of the network of hardware—computers

Father of the Web

Tim Berners-Lee was born in London, England, in 1955 to mathematician parents who worked on Harvard University's famous Mark I computer in the 1940s. He started writing computer languages in college and went on to hold several telecommunications jobs. He found that although the Internet was growing, it was difficult for users to find specific information. He crafted a solution for the problem, using documents written in something he called hypertext. These hypertext documents could be linked to other documents based on similar words. Berners-Lee also created a computer language called hypertext transfer protocol (HTTP) that all computers could use to transmit documents over the Internet. He invented a naming system for a hypertext document as well: the universal resource locator (URL). He even wrote the hypertext markup language (HTML) used to format documents to be shared online. He named the entire system the World Wide Web and made it available to the public in 1990.

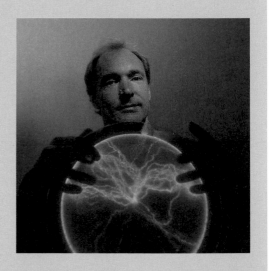

Sir Tim Berners-Lee invented the World Wide Web, a navigation system for the Internet, in 1990.

In 2004, Queen Elizabeth II knighted Berners-Lee father of the World Wide Web for his contribution to science and technology. By giving Internet users a simple way to find and share information, Berners-Lee's invention changed the world.

and the wires connecting them—and also the computer language of protocol that all connected devices can understand. Together, these create a vast world of online communication that has laid the groundwork for the existence of schools in the virtual realm of the Internet.

Organizing the Net

The Internet has made communication possible like no other development in the history of mankind. But its vast size can make the Internet overwhelming and difficult to use. Part of the complexity is that computers, not people, speak Internet protocol. To make computers and the Internet more user-friendly, especially for learners and instructors who wanted to exchange information online, it was necessary to develop a way for people to search the Internet in languages they *could* understand.

The World Wide Web has resolved some issues that arise from the sheer massiveness of the Internet. The web, as it is known, is one way of accessing and sorting through all the information on the Internet. The web operates like an Internet accessory. It uses its own protocol, called hypertext markup language (HTML), which is just one of many Internet languages. Navigating the web requires a special computer program, or software, called a web browser (like Firefox or Internet Explorer) that understands this protocol. The browser allows a computer user to type information requests in languages people understand, rather than numerical addresses. "In a world of people and information, the people and information should be in some kind of equilibrium," says Tim Berners-Lee. "The web should be a medium of communication between people."[17] Learners of all ages, from preschool to college, turn to the Internet as a learning resource, and web browsers are so user-friendly that even people with very few computer skills can use them to navigate HTML protocol and find information about almost anything they want to know.

Computer users can also use HTML protocol to add information to the web, not just retrieve it. They can set up their own original pages, or destinations, on the web.

An address for these destinations can be typed in—for example, www.google.com—and an information request moves along the pathways of the Internet to find the specific web page a user is looking for. In schools, this allows teachers to set up information pages, or websites, for their students to access. To find more general information on a topic, students can also use a special type of website called a search engine to find sites related to a specific topic or keyword. Web technology makes it possible for schools to exist online in the form of web pages and for students to search beyond their teachers' sites for additional information or new perspectives on whatever topics they like.

A person searches the Internet using Google, a popular search engine.

Data Speedways

Web pages were an amazing innovation because they allowed for a limitless supply of easily accessible information, something never before available to mankind. Those early web pages mostly consisted of text, colored backgrounds, and perhaps some photos or drawings. From an educational standpoint, they were an incredible learning opportunity, but since then, they have become much more complex. Today's web pages include animation, videos, sound, interactive tasks like games, message boards, chat rooms where people can talk in real time or even see each other on the screen, and hyperlinks that take users to other pages on a site or to other sites entirely. Such changes have made websites so useful and interactive as a teaching tool that many traditional textbooks now include website addresses where students can go online to experience virtual content that relates to the textbook's topics.

For online education to reach its full potential, websites must pass along vast amounts of data, and most online students and teachers rely on high-speed Internet connections, another name for broadband connections, to take advantage of all the features the Internet is capable of. The process of information exchange works a lot like roadways. Roads carry traffic between locations, and traffic laws make sure all drivers follow the same rules to get around safely. Automobiles act like the parcels of information, called packets, which pass back and forth along the wires of the Internet.

When a computer accesses the Internet, it sends out a request for information. It does so under a name—an Internet protocol (IP) address—that identifies the specific computer doing the asking and where that computer is located. The request, spoken in protocol, travels the wires until it reaches a router, which is another piece of physical hardware—a computer component whose job is to direct Internet traffic and prevent traffic jams. The router joins two or more networks. It listens to each information request that comes its way and sends the request to the address of the computer that can respond to it. Usually, a router must send the request toward another network, where another router may send the same request (or information packet) in a new direction.

"The router handles the packet by

A router is an essential component of smooth, fast Internet access. It directs Internet traffic, finding the quickest possible route for information to travel.

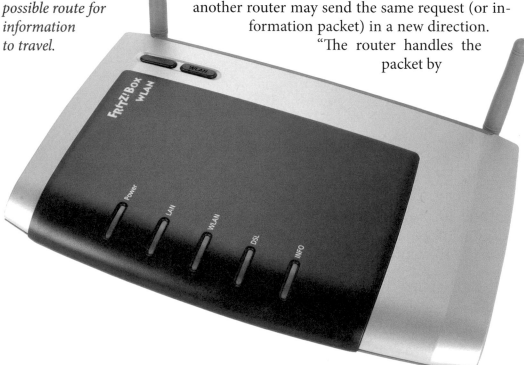

Inside a Wireless Router

Students of online schools can take laptops and other devices with them and access school wherever there is a wireless router: a device that sends and receives data from nearby computers and wireless devices to a modem that connects to the Internet with a wire. Common routers are rectangular with two plastic-coated antennae jutting from the top, which are used to send and receive data over radio waves. A wireless router also has connection ports, slots that link it by wires to a device with a wired connection to the Internet. The wireless router creates a hotspot, a place where nearby computers can exchange information with the router by the radio waves sent and received with its antennae. The router uses radio frequencies to broadcast the Internet signal to computers within its range. It works like a mix of a traditional modem and a cell phone. It allows nearby users to browse the web wirelessly, although not limitlessly—they have to stay in range of the router's antennae in order to stay connected to the Internet.

looking at the destination address and sending it to the neighboring router closer to the destination address," say physicists Romualdo Pastor-Satorras and Alessandro Vespignani. That is, the router sends the packet on "the best *next hop* toward the final destination."[18]

Routers are like traffic directors, showing every request or packet of information where to go but also where *not* to go. Routers serve the important function of sending information in the right direction by the fastest route. If one information roadway, or network, has heavy traffic, the router will send the message—such as a student question—in a different direction. And once the information request arrives at its destination, the answering computer's response—such as a teacher's explanation—may come back through the network following a completely different path, depending on which roadways are most congested. "This means that if a site is not working properly, or if it is too slow, data packets can be rerouted on the spot, somewhere else,"[19] say Pastor-Satorras and Vespignani. Routers eliminate what might otherwise be annoying delays in the transfer of information between online teachers and their students during hours when many people tend to use the Internet at the same time.

A computer's information request usually reaches its Internet destination—and the receiving computer sends back the response—in a few seconds. Through the Internet, computers exchange information with tremendous speed. A teacher can ask a question and a student can answer that question as quickly as sound travels, even if the two are in different cities, states, or countries. For education and learning, the benefits of the Internet are obvious. Student "askers" can be connected to instructor "responders" and get answers to questions on any subject about as quickly as if the two people were talking face-to-face.

Data packets, the information compressed by a computer to be passed along in small units and reassembled by the receiving computer, now bypass the traditional phone lines that were their original roadways. Instead, data travels along dedicated broadband Internet cables. These transport more data packets far more quickly than phone lines, much like a five-lane freeway allows more efficient travel than a two-lane country road. High-tech broadband wires move the huge volume of data that today's world demands at speeds that are acceptable to users. "Broadband connections are the railroads of the 21st century—essential infrastructure required to transmit products (these days, in the form of information),"[20] say the editors of *Scientific American* magazine.

A New Way to Communicate

The kind of data that gets transferred through high-speed Internet connections has evolved along with the wires themselves. Although typing and reading are still common means of communication between computer users, it is also possible to actually talk over the Internet. This requires technology called Voice over Internet Protocol, or VoIP.

HOW VOICE OVER INTERNET PROTOCOL (VoIP) WORKS

VoIP converts voice and sound into digital signals that travel over the Internet. The signals are sent as numbered "packets" to the remote computer. To recreate the sound, the destination computer sorts the packets and plays back the packets that are received. The packets are routed over the Internet one at a time; during this process, some may be delayed or lost in transmission. The VoIP process was later adapted for transmitting data and video, which revolutionized communication over the Internet.

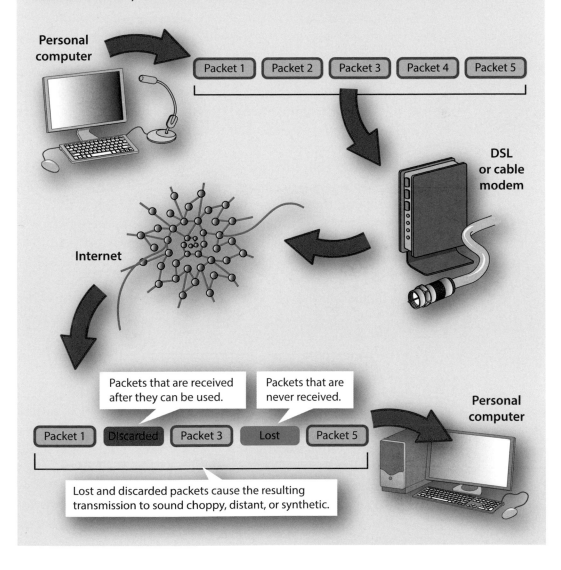

Personal computer

Packet 1 | Packet 2 | Packet 3 | Packet 4 | Packet 5

DSL or cable modem

Internet

Packets that are received after they can be used.

Packets that are never received.

Personal computer

Packet 1 | Discarded | Packet 3 | Lost | Packet 5

Lost and discarded packets cause the resulting transmission to sound choppy, distant, or synthetic.

With VoIP, two or more users can have actual conversations through their computers. Teachers can use VoIP to speak to their classes, and students can ask questions verbally. Teachers and students located anywhere in the world can speak to each other through a computer with an Internet connection.

Most modern computers are equipped with microphones that can record voices. A user at one computer can speak into his microphone, and VoIP will break the sounds down into tiny pieces of data. These are packaged into packets and, like all other information, passed along the Internet wires to the destination computer or website. There, the computer uses special protocol to reassemble the packets into the sound of the original speaker's voice. The process happens almost instantaneously.

Using concepts similar to VoIP, computer users can now use computer-based cameras as well as microphones, allowing them to see *and* hear each other while having a conversation through Skype or similar computer programs. Such technology has become a popular way for people to communicate all around the world, including in online classrooms. "We see now that the Internet is a much more efficient infrastructure for any kind of communications, be it voice, text, video, or whatever," says Niklas Zennström, co-founder of the VoIP Skype software program. "Certainly at some point the Internet will carry the majority of communication."[21]

VoIP especially enhances online schools, the virtual equivalent of a physical school building. Students in online schools can hear and see their teachers on their computer screens. Online learning was once considered solitary and lonely, with most interaction taking place through the keyboard. Gone are the days of silent online schools, as well as solitary learning. VoIP helps make an online school interactive, much like a classroom in a physical, brick-and-mortar school.

Math Tubs
Tub 1-5 Tub 6-2
Tub 2-6 Tub 7-1
Tub 3-4
Tub 5-3

Block Tubs
Mega Blocks - 2
Lincoln Logs - 3
Tinker Toys - 4
Legos   - 5
Wood Blocks - 6
Pattern Blocks -1

Communication technology has changed the entire concept of learning. As technology continues to evolve, it will bring new capabilities to users all around the world. Computer, Internet, and cell phone technology now let on-line students take the school "building" along with them wherever they go. For students and teachers all over the world, the Internet is redefining the experience of education by giving it a new setting in a digital space.

Kindergarten students in Hutchinson, Kansas, interact with students their age in Seoul, South Korea. The interaction is made possible by VoIP technology.

CHAPTER 3

Navigating an Online School

Anywhere students and teachers can access the Internet, they can now attend school. "Across the board you have without a doubt a technological movement in this country," says John G. Flores, CEO of the United States Distance Learning Association in Boston. "Distance learning is not only impacting education reform and education change, but more importantly, it's giving students new options they've never had before."[22] Even with all these new options, however, each online school has a unique structure and design. They have unique names, themes, school colors, even school mascots. Most keep official school hours and abide by school-year calendars.

Even though online schools provide more flexibility than brick-and-mortar schools, they are not independent of the school system. They still require students to spend the same amount of time learning, listening to lectures, taking tests, participating in class discussions, and even working together on group projects. Online schools are still schools. They just remove the physical walls and replace them with computer technology.

Learning on Site

Just as a traditional school day begins with students showing up for classes, a typical online school day also has opening rituals. Students turn on a computer, go online, and enter the web address of the online school. The virtual school experience comes from a web server, a special computer that sends specific programs or applications to users that request them. Servers share information with user computers using Internet protocol. When students' computers contact the online school server, it sends back the information they need for their school day.

The server is not only the source of the school's programs and classes, it also stores data about each student, including which lessons they have completed and which lessons remain incomplete. The server is the common contact point for all students and teachers participating in the school. A server stores a vast amount of data, much like a traditional school stores files on each student and teachers fill binders with lesson plans. When students in the online school enter the school's web address, they see the home page, the virtual equivalent of a school building's front door. Students must log in with a student name and password. This security measure has two functions—it tells the server which student is entering and the specific information that student needs for the day, such as the class schedule. It also makes sure that only registered students access the online school.

Once students have logged into the school's website, their classes may come up as a to-do list, with links to each class. When a student clicks on a link, the server sends that student to the class page and provides the information needed for that particular subject. The server may also track the student's attendance and progress in school. It can record the date and time that the student logged in and out. It may also record which links were accessed for which subjects.

Servers like this one are used by online schools to share information, store data, take attendance, track skills, and perform the many tasks required for online education.

The server stores all of this data for every student, which helps teachers keep track of student participation and progress. "Teachers take attendance, review student history, issue grades and credits, track skills, request certificates and even register students from any computer via the Web,"[23] says the website of Administrative Software Applications, which produces programs that can take classroom attendance online. Using such software, teachers and administrators of online schools can see at a glance which students log into school each day, what work they do, and how long they stay. It is almost as hard to be truant from an online school as it is from a regular brick-and-mortar classroom.

Anytime Lessons

Simply logging onto the school server for the required number of hours each day does not ensure that students are learning. Online schools provide actual lessons over the computer, and they do so in ways that can be much more interesting and engaging than in a traditional classroom. When students click on a link that takes them to the content of a particular lesson, it might be an actual recorded lecture from the teacher, which the student downloads as a video with sound and watches at a convenient time. Students can even watch recorded lectures more than once, which is one advantage of an online school.

Recorded lectures are an example of asynchronous lessons. "*Asynchronous e-learning*, commonly facilitated by media such as e-mail and discussion boards, supports work relations among learners and with teachers, even when participants cannot be online at the same time,"[24] says computer science researcher Stefan Hrastinski. One student might listen to the lecture at eight o'clock in the morning. Another might hear the same lecture after lunch. Both have the same access to the lecture—the only difference is the time of day they choose to listen.

Online schools use many forms of asynchronous lessons, not just recorded lectures from teachers. By clicking on a lesson link, a student might find written material that

A World of Webinars

Not all online learning happens in an online school. Private companies and organizations worldwide are using school-designed tools and programs like Blackboard to hold webinars—seminars or conferences conducted on the web. A webinar has many advantages over a traditional meeting or conference. Speakers can give their entire presentation or lecture, enhanced by slides, for attendees to see and hear on a computer. Attendees can be anywhere to get the information, so the number of attendees at a webinar is not limited by the size of a room. Companies can charge people to sign up for the webinar using computer programs that only let them log on once they have registered. Attendees benefit, too, because they do not have to pay travel costs or take time off of work to attend (they could watch a work-related webinar right from their office). Webinars are the modern versions of seminars and conferences, and they are cousins of online schools. Both use technology to bring people together to learn.

works something like an online textbook—it has text and photographs to explain a concept in history or science, for example. Students can move through this material at a comfortable pace and can even repeat a lesson if necessary. In an online school, asynchronous learning is self-paced and available to students at any time that they want to work on classes. "Many people take online courses *because* of their asynchronous nature," says Hrastinski. "Asynchronous e-learning makes it possible for learners to log on to an e-learning environment at any time and download documents or send messages to teachers or peers. Students may spend more time refining their contributions, which are generally considered more thoughtful compared to synchronous communication."[25]

Class Starts Promptly at Nine

Online schools also give students and teachers the option of attending synchronous class sessions—classes in which students and the teacher all meet in the same virtual classroom at the same time. A web server acts as the host for the synchronous classroom. At a specific time, students and the teacher log into a special site. They use microphones and sometimes cameras on their computers to record their voice or their image and send it over the Internet using Voice over Internet Protocol (VoIP). Everyone else in the classroom can hear or even see the person speaking on their computers. Teachers use this technology to give lectures in real time. Students can ask questions and share their own thoughts and ideas during these synchronous sessions.

Some software programs are designed specifically for synchronous sessions in online schools. One example is Blackboard, named after the chalkboards at the front of most traditional brick-and-mortar classrooms. Blackboard gives online teachers the same tools they would have if they were standing in a physical classroom to teach—they can explain concepts, write, draw, and present slideshows. Students can raise their hands by clicking a button on screen that alerts the teacher if someone has a question. Polling tools allow teachers to ask multiple-choice questions and get instant feedback as students choose A, B, C, or D. The program records student answers, making it possible to give pop quizzes in real time online. Students can write, draw, or type using Blackboard, too, sharing their ideas with the rest of the class.

Using tools like Blackboard, students and teachers can be in the same virtual place at the same time, even if they live far apart from each other. Economist Gerald W. Stone says that such programs give teachers and students "cutting-edge online materials that facilitate critical thinking and learning. . . . The result: an interactive, comprehensive online course."[26]

Interactive Classrooms

Lessons in online schools use sound and video frequently, and this allows them to do things a textbook cannot. Rather than just viewing a photograph of a historical event, students may view actual video footage of it, complete with sound. They might be able to see and hear a famous civil rights speech by Martin Luther King Jr., for example, instead of just reading the words. Online lessons might include links to external sources of information, such as online encyclopedias or the web page of a related museum. The lessons are interactive, allowing students to move forward or backward through the content at their own pace. With online classes, students can take the time to explore concepts that interest them and follow links for more information.

Online lessons are interactive in other ways, too. They often include animations to explain concepts. In geometry, for example, students may practice rotating shapes and taking measurements on screen. Students can play games in

Students participate in a class discussion with an instructor via videoconference. Synchronous online sessions allow students and teachers to meet in real time over the Internet.

an online school to help them memorize facts and practice concepts. They might create charts or graphs on their computers to organize facts and information. Virtual flashcards help students memorize rules or definitions. Lesson elements are combined with color, illustration, music, and sound effects to make them interesting and appealing to learners of all ages.

A tablet computer displays the online version of the Encyclopedia Britannica, *which was first published in 1771 and printed its last thirty-two-volume print edition in 2010. Links to online encyclopedias are often part of online lessons.*

Lesson designers who help create the content for online schools include graphic artists and other creative designers who work together to ensure that online lessons are informative, interesting, and fun for students. With streaming sound and video segments, visual and sound effects, games, and activities, online schools become exciting multimedia centers of learning, often personalized to students' needs and interests. "Endless possibilities are available for presenting educational content through text, audio, video, animations and interactions to create meaningful learning environments," says instructional web designer Eli Collins-Brown. "Such an incorporation of media can be used to address a variety of learning styles."[27]

Simulated Experiences

Interactive, multimedia technology provides students with the ability to participate in virtual replacements of the real-life experiences available in traditional classrooms. Science laboratories, for example, can be recreated in a virtual setting. In a high school chemistry class, for example, students might fill glass test tubes and beakers with chemicals and then mix substances together to observe the reactions. Chemistry students in online schools can also participate in laboratory experiments—by computer, choosing which chemicals and how much of each to add to test tubes and

Becoming a Graphic Designer

Job description: Graphic designers use computer software, photographs, drawings, and other artistic tools to create the visual elements of publications and, increasingly, websites. Online schools frequently use graphic designers to help make the content of their courses fun and appealing for learners.

Education: Graphic designers need to complete at least a certificate program or bachelor's degree in graphic design before looking for a job. A bachelor's degree may improve job prospects. Some graphic design programs are now available from online schools.

Qualifications: Job candidates create a portfolio of their best design work to show employers or clients. Graphic designers must demonstrate that they are creative, patient, and good at problem solving. They also must be able to understand and follow directions to create graphic designs that will please clients.

Additional Information: Graphic designers usually start with an entry-level job in advertising, publishing, or website design and work their way up. About one-third of graphic designers are self-employed.

Salary: $40,000 per year and up.

A pilot trains in a flight simulator. Simulated training and education have become increasingly commonplace, and many argue that simulated learning is just as valuable as real-life experience.

then which tubes to mix. If their choices are correct, the computer will animate the reaction—the mixture bubbling or changing colors, for example.

Subjects such as biology are well suited to online simulations, too. Dissecting a virtual frog with virtual scalpels and probes rather than real ones is one activity that students can complete online. The computer simulation might include sounds and even zoom in to reveal the frog's organs once the student makes a virtual incision. Students' progress can be tracked by computer, and mistakes, such as misplaced incisions, can be noted. The computer can provide feedback to the teacher about students who need extra help and analyze mistakes on a simulated experiment.

Science classes with virtual laboratories are sometimes criticized for not giving online students the same experiences students would have in a real classroom. However, as technology continues to improve, virtual simulations are becoming important training tools, not just in high schools and universities, but in real-world jobs. Airline pilots receive a significant part of their training in flight simulators, for example. The mining industry uses simulations to train employees in disaster preparedness. Meteorologists use computerized simulation programs to practice predicting and forecasting weather outcomes. Even doctors increasingly use computer-based simulations to practice performing surgeries or making medical decisions based on data from various test results.

Simulated laboratory experiments in online schools use some of the same technology students might one day encounter in their actual careers—and studies indicate that computer simulations are effective learning tools. According to the University of Central Florida's Institute for Simulation and Training:

> Because they can recreate experiences, simulations hold great potential for training people for almost any situation. Education researchers have, in fact, determined that people, especially adults, learn better by experience than through reading or lectures. Simulated experiences can be just as valuable a training tool as the real thing.[28]

Simulations are one of the many technological tools used by online schools to teach students a variety of subjects entirely over the Internet.

No More Number Two Pencils

Just as online schools take attendance and deliver lessons in a variety of ways, they can also assess how well students are learning. Many online schools have an e-mail system built into the school's web server. This allows teachers and students to exchange e-mails with one another through the school's private program. Students can type a report or an essay on their computer using word-processing software, then upload the document into the e-mail program and send it to their teacher. The date stamp on the e-mail tracks whether the student turned in the assignment on time. The teacher downloads students' e-mailed documents to a personal computer to read and grade them.

Pack It Up

In order to transfer data along Internet wires or over cell phone radio waves, the transmitting device must first break the information into many small pieces, or packets. The packets are then sent along piece by piece to the receiving computer. Using protocol, or a special computer language, the receiving computer or device determines what to do with the incoming packets. The process works like a digital jigsaw puzzle. The piece of data to be sent—such as a verbal conversation, a visual image, video footage, or a school paper sent as a document—is broken into small pieces that are part of the whole. These pieces are then sent along to the receiving device, which collects them, in no particular order, and reassembles them back into a recognizable image, document, or sound. Sometimes, pieces are lost along the way, so a sending computer may make copies of each puzzle piece and send them all. The receiving computer discards unnecessary duplicates. Because each packet, or puzzle piece, is just a small part of the whole, the receiving computer, phone, or other device is able to fill in the gaps if a small piece of data does not arrive.

Online schools are well equipped to let students use special computer tools and software to enhance papers and reports; students might add graphs, charts, or data tables into their projects, for example. In art courses, students may produce a drawing or painting at home on paper. They then might use a digital scanner, a device that works like a photocopy machine, to save the copy to their computer as a digital file. Students can upload and e-mail the scanned image, in full color, just as they would share any other document. Photographs of projects or of students completing assignments can be taken too, often by cell phone, and e-mailed directly to a teacher. Computers, tablets, cell phones, and other devices can all be used for turning in homework and projects to teachers online, in a variety of formats. The technological abilities online schools give to students for preparing assignments are so successful that many brick-and-mortar schools also encourage their students to use the kinds of software programs that online students use every day.

Even classes that require a great deal of interaction between students and teachers, such as music, public speaking, or foreign languages, can be assessed in an online school. Students can sing or play an instrument using a microphone while the teacher listens or record and send video footage of their performances. A student might use a computer microphone to speak to an online classroom filled with peers in order to practice delivering speeches in front of a crowd or complete an assignment by recording a speech delivered to a club, church group, or other gathering of people. A teacher can listen to foreign language students reading or speaking online and give pointers about improving pronunciation. The technology now exists to allow students to take courses online that were once difficult or impossible to carry out with distance education.

Tests and quizzes may be the easiest form of assessment the online school provides. Multiple-choice and fill-in-the-blank tests can be completed entirely on the school's web server. Entire tests or certain questions on a test can be timed, if necessary, which serves to discourage students from looking up answers. Exams completed online can also be graded by the computer system. This allows teachers to spend more time creating lessons and helping students and less time grading tests. With computer grading and feedback, students can also find out immediately how they scored on a test and what questions they missed.

Learning Management Systems, or software programs that help teachers administer and track online learning

Video conferencing has made it easy for students to visually communicate across the globe.

courses and assessments, can also organize test results into charts, graphs, or tables, allowing teachers to check comprehension of one student or the class as a whole about certain questions or topics. This helps teachers adapt their teaching methods or focus on concepts that are most challenging for students. Computerized testing in online schools is often more efficient and effective than the pencil-and-paper tests common in traditional classrooms, so much so that even traditional schools are having students complete assessments online. "There have been serious discussions at the U.S. Department of Education about moving all testing to an online format," says education professor Kris Sloan. "Rather than issuing students a paper test to be filled out with the familiar number two pencil, students would take tests at computers."[29] Grading students' work is one more way online schools are setting trends that traditional schools might one day follow.

Libraries in the Online School

Lessons, tests, group projects, and socializing with teachers and fellow students can all occur virtually in an online school, even without a physical school building for students to attend each day. A central element of any brick-and-mortar school, however, is the library, the place where students traditionally go to do their research. Online schools lack a place to store all the books, newspapers, magazines, and other resources typically held by a school library. This does not mean online schools lack libraries, though. In fact, digital libraries are also evolving rapidly. Because so many Internet users now read content on a computer or handheld device instead of in print, most magazines and newspapers offer digital online versions of subscriptions to their publications. They may sell such subscriptions to online schools to provide students with access to digital periodicals.

Increasingly, book publishers are also creating digital versions of their books. These versions can be read on e-readers such as the Amazon Kindle or the Barnes and Noble Nook but also on any computer or mobile device as long as us-

ers download the reading software. Most e-books are available only to purchase, so online schools may have limited e-books to lend to students at no cost. However, they may also partner with public libraries that do offer digital books and materials that can be borrowed and downloaded with a computer.

Colleges and universities with online degree programs also offer access to their full library system and may even ship books and other library materials to online students who wish to borrow them. Many online schools make up for the lack of a physical library building by subscribing to information databases. Students can log in and access these databases from their computers for full-text versions of thousands of magazines, journals, and books.

Libraries still remain a centralized hub of information and learning resources, but the Internet makes it possible for students to access more of these resources without visiting a physical library building. They can use digital search tools to see what resources libraries have available and can

An Amazon Kindle e-reader, shelved amid a number of paperbacks, displays the cover of a Jules Verne book. E-readers have become increasingly popular for educational uses, and libraries often will make them available for student use.

often borrow them, all from a distance. Modern librarians, many of whom are now called media specialists, can communicate over the Internet with online students and help these learners sort through a sometimes overwhelming amount of information to find high-quality sources in print or digital form. "Although a lot of information is free online, it is not necessarily accurate and complete information," says Michael Dula, chief technology officer for the Yale University Library. "Librarians are well suited to help people to navigate and identify credible electronic data."[30]

Education, information, and communication are all going digital, making libraries and their information more accessible to distance learners. "A big part of what libraries do is purchase electronic resources to make them available to our patrons for free,"[31] Dula says. Online students at colleges and universities have the same access to the school's library resources as students taking classes in traditional classrooms, but even schools that lack their own brick-and-mortar version of a library can partner with public libraries.

Reaching the Full Potential of Learning

Just as the role of librarians is changing in an increasingly digital world, the roles of teachers and students are changing as well. Students still need to learn facts and practice skills, but more than just memorizing information, they need to learn how to find and sort out high-quality information—skills that will help them thrive in a digital world in the future. Teachers must be willing to adapt their teaching practices to reflect the needs of online classroom environments. Online schools give teachers a wealth of new ways to present subjects and content. "The Internet and other communications tools open up vast opportunities," say education specialists Kevin Ryan and James M. Cooper. "Compare assigning a sterile textbook article about French food to connecting your students with e-pals in French-speaking [countries in] Africa so they can ask about the cuisine themselves."[32]

The Internet makes possible many creative teaching ideas that until recent decades were impractical. To take advantage of these, teachers often must see themselves not as dispensers of information but as coaches who connect students with the huge variety of learning opportunities now available online. It is a different way of teaching and learning, and often considered a nontraditional one, but it is catching on around the world.

CHAPTER 4

Drawbacks of Online Learning

Virtual schools are growing rapidly both in size and number. As digital technology advances, Internet-connected devices seem to be everywhere, and the demand for online learning has exploded. The ability to attend school from almost any place and at any time appeals to many students. In a world in which people are surrounded with digital media in the form of television, video games, online chatting, and social media sites, online schools seem to be a logical direction for the field of education.

There is disagreement, however, about whether online schools are as effective as traditional brick-and-mortar schools. Online schools are a subject of controversy among educators, students, and society as a whole. Traditional schools in the United States have operated in much the same way for more than a century; time has proven that certain methods of instruction work well. Many generations of students have graduated from traditional schools, gotten jobs, and experienced success in the adult world. Teaching practices often differ in online schools, and because they are so new, it is too soon to compare the success of students who have been schooled in this way to the success of students who have graduated from traditional institutions.

Many people question whether online schools do an adequate job of preparing students for real life. "To the best of our knowledge, there is no compelling evidence that online learning systems available today . . . can in fact deliver improved educational outcomes across the board,"[33] say researchers at Ithaka, a New York–based nonprofit organization that studies digital learning.

Attendance Struggles

One serious concern about online schools has been the perception that it is too easy and tempting for students to skip class or apply little effort. This has always been a criticism of correspondence education in general, and online schools are often perceived as computerized versions of the correspondence classes of old. Traditional schools require students to be present in the school building every day. Teachers take attendance, and students who arrive late to class, or not at all, suffer consequences. Every state has a law that requires minors under age eighteen to attend school during school hours, unless that student has

A special education teacher in Macon, Georgia, gives one-on-one attention to a student. Many argue that online schools make it more difficult to forge the important relationship between teacher and student.

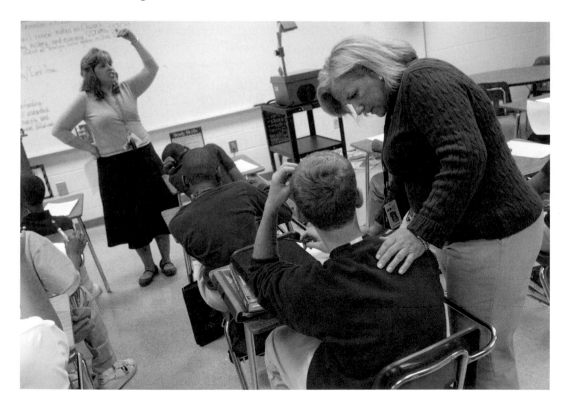

parental permission to be absent and a legitimate excuse such as illness.

Time spent in a classroom, seated at a desk, listening to and looking at a teacher has always been considered an important part of learning. "The heart of the classroom is found in the unique relationships between students and teachers," says U.S. Secretary of Education Arne Duncan. "In the same way that a family turns a house into a home, a physical and emotional transformation takes place when teachers and students work together in community to reach common goals."[34] Online schools, however, make it harder for teachers to know their students, to determine who is in class and is paying attention, and to know how long students actually spend studying.

Asynchronous classes, those that can be completed at a student's convenience, are especially difficult to monitor. Students may be able to check in, click assignments as "done," and check back out after only a few minutes in a class that is expected to take an hour or more. They may spend just one or two total hours a day attending school, compared to the six or more hours traditional students attend a brick-and-mortar building. Online school servers attempt to monitor attendance by keeping track of when students log in and out of classes and tallying up the number of hours spent online. But if students log in, then watch TV or do something else for an hour before logging out, they have not spent the time paying attention and learning.

Synchronous classes, ones in which the teacher holds sessions with a specific start time and students must join the online room to be counted as present, follow the model of traditional school more closely. The server keeps track of who logs in and out, and teachers can call on specific students to respond to questions using their microphone. This helps ensure that students are actually in front of their computer and paying attention during class. Even so, teachers cannot see students and have no way of knowing whether someone is dozing off, reading a book, playing video games, or even talking on the phone while logged into the classroom.

MOST SCHOOL DISTRICTS USE ASYNCHRONOUS INSTRUCTION FOR DISTANCE LEARNING

Asynchronous Internet courses are by far the most common type of technology used by U.S. public school districts that have distance education programs.

The graphs below show the percentage of U.S. public school districts with students enrolled in a particular mode of distance learning in the 2009–2010 school year.

One-way prerecorded video
2%

Two-way interactive video
17%

Computer-based (non-Internet)
5%

Asynchronous Internet courses
63%

Synchronous Internet courses
14%

Synchronous refers to simultaneous or "real time" instruction. Asynchronous refers to instruction not occurring in real time. Computer-based technologies include internal district networks or CD-ROM. Two-way interactive video includes two-way audio. One-way prerecorded video includes videos and DVDs, as well as television and cable broadcasts.

Data taken from: Barbara Queen and Laurie Lewis, *Distance Education Courses for Public Elementary and Secondary School Students: 2009–2010.* Washington, D.C.: U.S. Department of Education, National Center for Education Statistics, 2011. http://nces.ed.gov/pubs2012/2012008.pdf.

The Downside of Too Much Freedom

Online schools are also sometimes criticized for the mobility they allow students. The convenience of going to class from a coffee shop or while on vacation appeals to many students, but some cannot handle the distractions that accompany such environments. It is hard for many students to focus on lessons when they are surrounded by interesting sounds, sights, and foods. Most online students find that to be successful in this school format, they need a single, quiet space such as an office or bedroom to do schoolwork without distractions. The convenience of completing lessons anywhere and anytime is often touted as a benefit of online school, but some students are unrealistic about the extent of their self-discipline. Many find that they learn more successfully with the daily structure and schedule of a traditional brick-and-mortar school.

Inside a Web Browser

The Internet is a worldwide network of computer connections. The World Wide Web, invented by Tim Berners-Lee, gives computers a special language for navigating the Internet and guidelines for creating Internet destinations, or web pages. A browser is a type of software that, when installed on a specific computer, lets it (and the computer's user) search the web by finding addresses and going to various pages.

There are many web browsers, such as Internet Explorer, Firefox, and Google Chrome. All have basically the same user-friendly components. They include an address bar where the user can type in a specific universal resource locator (URL) for the desired website. *Back* and *forward* buttons take the user to pages previously viewed. *Refresh* and *stop* buttons reload a website or stop the loading process. A *home* button takes the browser back to the user's preferred starting page. Beneath these components, called the user interface, the browser has mechanisms that communicate the user's requests over the Internet and bring back the requested information, displaying it on the computer screen. Browsers are complicated software, but as the typical "face" of the Internet, users almost think of their browser, the Internet, and the web as one and the same.

Online students may spend as much time on schoolwork as students in traditional classrooms, but the online school format requires a high level of responsibility and self-motivation. Students may suffer from the lack of reminders and the ability to check in with teachers that take place in a traditional school. It is possible to succeed and even thrive in such a setting, but online school does not work well for everyone.

High school or college students who are easily distracted or are not very self-motivated can falter under the lenient online system. Elementary-aged students are even more vulnerable. Most young students require the near-constant supervision of a parent or other adult who stays with them during their school hours and makes sure they attend their classes and complete their schoolwork on time. "I wasn't always a person who used time wisely, who was as structured as maybe I should be," says Bill Holland, a graduate of an online university. "It's almost like the freedom you have with online classes is either going to bring out the best or the worst in you."[35] Online schools still struggle more than traditional, brick-and-mortar schools with regulating the time and effort students devote to their studies.

Negative Stereotypes

Students of online schools who attend class in a coffee shop or at a park on a sunny day may not seem to be taking school seriously, and this perception contributes to a low regard for online learning. Students and teachers in traditional schools often claim that completing online classes is easier than attending lectures, taking in-class tests, doing homework, and handing in papers and reports. Cheating is a constant concern.

Teachers cannot tell whether students taking tests from their home computer might be glancing at notes or flipping through their textbooks for answers. A friend in the same room could be giving hints. Teachers who might live hundreds of miles away have few ways to monitor students. Online students may graduate from programs with excellent grades but have cheated on some of their schoolwork. "Virtual schools offer much greater opportunity for students to obtain credit for work they did not do themselves,"[36] says the National Education Policy Center. It is considered harder to get away with cheating in a traditional school, where students are under nearly constant supervision in the classroom.

Not all online schools and programs are of the same quality. Some, particularly at the college level, advertise themselves as educational shortcuts, offering students a diploma, degree, or certification in a fraction of the time and with much less work. Some schools that make such claims are frauds. Students pay for the program, only to find that once the work is completed and the tuition paid, the promised diploma or degree is not recognized by employers or by

Online education allows students to complete assignments and study almost anywhere, in groups or alone. For these reasons, critics claim that online courses cannot be as challenging as traditional ones.

other schools. Such institutions have been called diploma mills, offering students credentials they have not really worked for. There are many examples of low-quality brick-and-mortar institutions that also offer shortcuts and easy routes to diplomas, and diploma mills have long plagued distance learning in general. But critics of nontraditional learning target online programs as the latest and easiest way to offer educational shortcuts to students.

Certainly not all online schools are of questionable quality, just as not all brick-and-mortar institutions are reputable. Both online classes and classes in traditional schools vary widely. Some online classes are even more rigorous than comparable classes in brick-and-mortar classrooms. As online learning institutions grow in number and popularity, however, questions about the relative quality of an online education and one obtained the traditional way will endure. "Although research has found no significant difference in learning outcomes through education obtained in DE (distance education) courses, resistance among students, faculty, and even politicians and employers still exists,"[37] says Clemson University Vice Provost Diane G. Smathers.

Faculty members and students of online schools often must work hard to overcome negative perceptions. However, to meet the needs and desires of students in grades K–12 and in college who want to fulfill some or all of their education requirements online, many schools with excellent reputations now offer at least some online courses, if not entire degree or diploma programs online. As time passes and society becomes more accustomed to online learning, it will become harder to find reasons to criticize a mode of education that is in high demand and has the potential to offer valuable opportunities to many students.

It Is a Steep Climb over the Digital Divide

The demand for online courses is growing rapidly, and more institutions are finding ways to offer reputable, rigorous digital distance learning. Nevertheless, certain people are unintentionally excluded from the academic benefits of online learning. Students in an online school require access to certain technology in order to attend classes. At the least, online students need a fairly modern computer, one that can play videos with sound and record the student's voice and image. Most online students also need a printer, a digital scanner, and modern software with features such as a word processor, a program to make spreadsheets, and a program to view and create slides for digital slideshows. They also need a way to access the Internet, preferably with a reliable, high-speed connection. Not everyone has equal access to these tools and resources, and therefore, online education is not equally available to all students who might want to try it.

One factor that puts online education out of reach for some students is cost. Equipment and software for taking online classes can be expensive. Internet and cellular service providers also charge customers for Internet connections and Internet-capable accessories, which result in monthly fees on top of the cost of equipment. Many states are setting up online charter schools that provide required computer equipment and Internet access to students at no cost, but state-funded education via computer is not yet available to everyone. "Online education," says attorney Edward Lin, "is failing to live up to its promise of providing greater opportunity for all. Fewer minority, lower-income, and special-education students attend online schools."[38]

Students' ability to afford technology gadgets is not the only obstacle that stands between them and online school. Internet and cell phone services are not always available, especially in rural areas. Most of the nation's cities and suburbs have broadband, high-speed Internet access. In very small towns, however, or in sparsely populated areas, cell towers may not be close enough to provide cellular service, and the Internet may be available only through dial-up phone lines. Slow-speed Internet connections like these may not be capable of carrying the large amount of data necessary to download videos and sound files quickly. Their characteristic slowness and delays may also prevent students from conversing in an online classroom in real time.

At the end of 2011, the Pew Research Center reported that 22 percent of American adults and 5 percent of American teenagers did not use the Internet with any device, whether by choice or because they had no access. According to the Federal Communications Commission (FCC), about 14 million Americans, or about 7 million U.S. households, were still without broadband Internet service as of 2011. This gap between Internet users and non-users has been called the United States' digital divide—a separation between those who have access to regular Internet service and those who do not. "The gap between the technological haves and have-nots, once defined by access to the computer hardware that drives high-tech learning, now centers on an information superhighway that too often recedes to the digital equivalent of rutted rural back roads,"[39] says Kevin Simpson, a reporter for the *Denver Post*.

Solitary Confinement

Lack of Internet access in isolated parts of the country makes it impossible for many people to attend online schools, but online schools can also *cause* isolation, even in highly populated areas. The U.S. school system has historically centered on classrooms where students spend their school days with peers. Even though wireless Internet access may allow students to venture out of their homes for school, they may by choice or for other reasons spend the entire school day alone, talking to no one face-to-face in real time.

Critics of online schooling regard this as a significant drawback. Most students in traditional schools enjoy interacting with their classmates and their teachers. School is the place where they make friends; it is often their primary social outlet. An online school, on the other hand, greatly reduces the opportunity for students to get to know one

Hidden Dangers of Virtual Learning

In many ways, online schools are safer than traditional schools. Schoolyard bullies, kidnappers, school shootings, and traffic accidents on the way to and from school do not exist online. However, just being online has dangers that are unique to that environment. Students who spend much of the day on the Internet could be at risk of identity theft if they download a computer virus or post personal or financial information on the wrong websites. Posting personal information, such as their name and address, might also make them targets of child predators. Online students also risk cyberbullying, which is the use of the Internet to post cruel comments about another person. Students who do not understand Internet rules and laws risk involvement in illegal activities such as piracy—downloading digital copyrighted content such as music or books without paying for them. Online students need to be aware of the risks, and many online schools include such instruction as part of their educational courses.

another. Even if they talk to each other and to teachers in online classrooms using microphones, they may live many miles apart and have few chances to meet. Many people consider a chat room to be a poor substitute for real friendship and social interaction. "Internet learning promises to make intellectual life more sterile and abstract than it already is," says English professor Mark Edmundson, "and also, for teachers and for students alike, far more lonely."[40]

There is some concern in society that young people already do not spend enough time talking to others and interacting in person. Kids, teens, and young adults spend a growing number of their daily hours cell-phone texting and visiting social media websites such as Facebook and Twitter and less time talking to people and socializing with friends face-to-face, according to the Kaiser Family Foundation, a nonprofit organization that studies health issues in the United States. The Kaiser Foundation also says that kids ages eight to eighteen spend an average of seven hours per day using media, which includes watching TV and videos, surfing the Internet, playing computer and video games, and listening to music. Young people growing up in a digital world spend far less time having real conversations with others than previous generations did.

Some social-development experts fear that online schools remove students' primary opportunities for socialization, replacing them with solitary hours spent on a computer or other device. As online learning becomes more common, future generations of students might miss out on important social-development experiences such as teamwork, sharing, learning to get along with others, and speaking to groups of peers. "Children need to learn the real social world before they learn the virtual one,"[41] says child-development professor David Elkind.

The use of social media—such as Facebook or Twitter—instead of having real-life interactions raises the concern that online students may be deprived of vital social-development experiences.

Staying Stationary

Students who attend online schools may live solitary lives compared to traditional students, and they also may live stationary ones. In a 2010 study of American students, the U.S. Centers for Disease Control (CDC) found that only 12 percent of all high school-age students get the recommended amount of exercise—sixty minutes of physical activity every day. Online students who spend a majority of their day sitting in front of a computer screen may get even less than that. Online schools make it possible for students to attend all of their classes without ever leaving their home, or even their bedroom. Students at brick-and-mortar schools, on the other hand, have chances to be active throughout the day, such as walking between classes and walking to and from school. Students in brick-and-mortar schools usually take physical education classes, as well, and many participate in after-school sports on campus.

Students who attend online schools might miss many of these built-in opportunities for physical activity and must make a conscious effort to exercise, because they might otherwise attend school for the entire day without ever leaving their chairs. Experts point out that both the health and academics of those who lack daily exercise may suffer. "Not only does recess aid personal development," says Elkind, "but studies have found that children who are most physically fit tend to score highest on tests of reading, math and science."[42]

Lack of physical activity has also been linked to obesity, a significant and growing health concern for the U.S. population in general and for children and teens especially. According to the CDC, about 20 percent of American children age eighteen or younger are considered obese, a number that has tripled in the past three decades. A sedentary lifestyle—meaning that a person spends most of the day sitting and gets very little physical activity—is considered a major cause of this rise in childhood and teen obesity. Many young people already spend most of their free time sitting to watch TV, use a computer, or play video games. Online schools potentially add to the problem. "Physical

Virtual P.E.

Physical education, or P.E., is one thing students cannot do online. Assigning and grading P.E. workouts for online students is harder than assigning academic work. Given the importance of daily exercise and an active lifestyle, however, many online schools have added this requirement. As with all subjects, teachers find creative ways to adapt P.E. for the online learner. One growing trend is to require activities such as swimming, walking, or yoga and move away from group sports like soccer and basketball that were once the mainstay of P.E. classes. Online P.E. classes can teach students proper exercises with photo and video tutorials. Students are then required to log the amount of time that they exercise, their pulse rate, and other factors.

The main benefit of an online P.E. course may be teaching students how to fit exercise time into their busy days and stick to their exercise schedules. Teenagers who develop healthy exercise habits are more likely to continue those habits as adults. Online P.E. courses teach students to take responsibility for choosing an enjoyable physical activity and regularly making time for it.

A woman practices yoga using an online tutorial. To promote physical activity, many online schools require physical education classes as part of their curriculum.

fitness and health are crucial, yet often neglected, elements in education," says online physical fitness instructor Katie Carone. "Most people have visions of fingers working vigorously as students click a computer mouse or video game their way to a sedentary lifestyle."[43]

It is also easy for an online student to snack all day, another obesity risk factor. In traditional schools, food

Teenagers dance at a high school prom. Online education lacks school traditions, such as dances and sporting events, that some feel are necessary for positive emotional growth and socialization.

and beverages are typically not allowed in the classroom. Students eat only at designated snack and lunch times. Students in an online school, however, have no definite meal schedule within their day. If they spend time in front of the computer consuming foods high in calories and low in nutrition, such as soda, candy, and potato chips, the risk of health problems and obesity increases.

Attending an online school does not necessarily mean that a student will develop more unhealthy habits than students in traditional schools. Indeed, many brick-and-mortar schools have also come under criticism for offering unhealthy lunch and snack options in the cafeterias, which contribute to student weight gain. However, healthy habits can be emphasized every day at traditional schools, whereas online schools have less influence over these areas of student life. Online school students must take it upon themselves or depend on parental guidance to avoid the pitfalls of too many snack foods and too little exercise.

A Loss of Traditions

Physical health is only one aspect of online schooling that critics highlight. School traditions such as pep rallies, student assemblies, elections for class officers, homecoming, prom, and signing yearbooks are considered healthy for students' emotional growth and become cherished memories once students graduate. However, these traditions are often missing from online schools.

The students in an online school may be spread out over a wide area, even crossing state or national borders. A group of students may interact online, but they are not likely to get together to play basketball or participate in a school play. Online students miss out on many of the social experiences people fondly associate with their years at a brick-and-mortar school. Some online schools organize sports teams or social events for students who live in the same area, but online students may be unable to attend or uninterested in participating. In fact, some students are not seeking, or may even be actively avoiding, the social community associated with traditional schools.

The limited opportunities to socialize, make friends among classmates, take part in extracurricular activities, and develop romantic relationships are considered by some to be major drawbacks of attending school online. While students who attend classes over the Internet may be satisfied with the overall academic experience, they may feel they are missing out on important social traditions. Online schools are new, and the technology that makes them possible is exciting, but many people worry that online schools are limiting students' lives in significant ways.

CHAPTER 5

Advantages of Virtual Classrooms

Attending school over the Internet is not for everyone, but the popularity of online schools is growing, and enrollment is increasing rapidly. According to the Center for Public Education, about 250,000 elementary-, middle-, and high-school students nationwide were enrolled in online schools as of 2012. Though this is a small percentage of the approximately 50 million total students enrolled in public schools nationwide, enrollment in online schools for grades kindergarten through twelve is increasing by 25 percent per year. If growth continues at this pace, online K–12 enrollment could surpass 1 million students by the year 2018.

Online learning is even more popular among students at colleges and universities. Post-secondary schools in the United States now enroll more than 6 million students—a third of all the college students in the United States—who attend at least one virtual class while they attend college. More than 1.25 million higher-education students attend all of their classes online.

The rapid growth of online education is evidence that many learners are attracted to this form of schooling. Though there are disadvantages to online education, students who try it often find that the positives outweigh the negatives. In a world that is increasingly digital, attend-

ing school online seems to be a natural mode of education for more learners. "They [young people] read blogs rather than newspapers. They often meet each other online before they meet in person," say John Palfrey and Urs Gasser of the Berkman Center for Internet and Society. "Major aspects of their lives—social interactions, friendships, civic activities—are mediated by digital technologies. And they've never known any other way of life."[44] Enrollment in online learning may eventually match or even overtake that in traditional brick-and-mortar schools as digital capabilities continue to transform the modern world.

Many students struggle with the pacing and difficulty of traditional education. Online learning provides flexibility and customization to individual students.

Education Tailored to the Learner

One reason online learning draws an increasing number of students is the flexibility it offers. For centuries, public school in the United States has occurred on weekdays, during prescribed hours, and with students typically grouped into classrooms with randomly selected peers their own

Internet Explorer Gets an Upgrade

As long as there have been web browsers—software that computers use to efficiently surf the web—there have been browser upgrades to enable users to surf faster, more efficiently, and with more user-friendly features. Internet Explorer (IE) was created by the Microsoft Corporation in 1995 and automatically installed as a default browser on new computers. Within months of its debut, a newer, faster, and better version of IE was released. In 2012, Microsoft released the ninth generation. Whereas earlier versions were often slow to load pages, IE 9 boasted loading speeds that rivaled the speed of programs installed on a computer's hard drive. IE 9 had other features, too; it allowed users to open favorite sites without opening the web browser first and to pause the downloading process and then continue from where it left off. IE 9, at the time of its development, was considered state of the art. As with all things Internet-related, however, it is only a matter of time until developers improve the browser once again.

age. Everyone in the class is expected to learn the same material in the same way at the same time. College and university courses offer somewhat more flexibility with evening and weekend classes, but students still need to be on campus and take their classes in a classroom.

Many students struggle with the rigid school hours and locations of traditional brick-and-mortar schools. Learners of all ages differ in personality and learning style. Some students are more focused and learn best early in the morning, whereas others do their best thinking in the afternoon or evening. Some students have disabilities that make it hard for them to get to school, sit in a room full of people, and focus on their studies. Some students work faster than their peers in certain subjects and therefore find traditional school boring as they wait for their peers to catch up, while other students may need to spend extra time on certain topics and struggle to keep up as the teacher and the rest of the class move on. Some students find brick-and-mortar schools to be a source of social problems, too—bullying, for example, affects a student's focus in the classroom and desire to go to school at all. According to the U.S. Department of Education, being bullied can lead to lower grades, less interest in one's academic and career future, and an increase in school absences. Bullied students in traditional classrooms often miss out academically.

Brick-and-mortar colleges can pose the same challenges as well as others. Many college students find that even with flexible scheduling of classes in the evenings and on weekends, attending college still requires them to move close to the campus of their choice, perhaps work only part-time, and spend many hours every day on campus for class. College attendance can be especially difficult for nontraditional students, typically older students who may already have full-time jobs and a family to support.

Online schools are a solution to many challenges of brick-and-mortar schools. Most offer true flexibility in scheduling with asynchronous learning, which allows students to access their courses any time of the day or week when they learn best or can fit school into their schedule. In an online school, students can also move at their own pace, going more quickly through material they understand and taking extra time on material that is harder for them. They avoid the social distractions of traditional classrooms, including bullying. College students can often complete their entire degree at a school of their choice without relocating to live near the campus. When college students are not required to commute to class, they can fit their courses into the hours of the day that work best around their job, family, or other obligations.

Online schools can tailor education to the needs and learning styles of each individual student, something that is more difficult for traditional brick-and-mortar schools to do. "Online learning reminds us that learning is not determined by where, but by how kids are taught," says Steve Perry, founder and principal of a magnet school in Connecticut. "Schooling is not place, it's a process."[45]

Expanding Resources

Another benefit of online schools is that they can extend the same learning opportunities to all students equally, something brick-and-mortar schools cannot always do. Rural areas, for example, might have very small schools

BITS & BYTES
70 percent
Proportion of community college students who say high-speed Internet access is essential to success in school (just 66 percent say access to professors is essential).

with few students, few teachers, and little diversity in course-work beyond the basic core subjects. Underprivileged areas with limited economic resources may have similar restrictions on the number and variety of courses they are able to offer to students, often focusing most of their resources on helping struggling students become proficient in core subjects like reading and math rather than offering advanced or specialized courses that might only interest a few students. "Online instruction is especially beneficial for students in rural or poor school districts that might not have access to advanced courses," say education specialists Allan Ornstein, Daniel Levine, and Gerald Gutek. "Also, a shortage of certified teachers in hard-to-staff subject areas might also necessitate. . .online courses."[46]

With advances in Internet technology and continuing improvements to Internet access, digital classrooms are rapidly becoming accessible to students from any region

A teacher in Beijing, China, teaches Mandarin Chinese to a student in another country via an interactive online lesson. Online schools offer an advantage for students who wish to study languages such as Chinese that are less frequently offered in traditional schools.

or district regardless of its funding or geographic location. Such online classes often have students from small country towns as well as large inner-city school districts. One teacher with training in a particular subject can serve the needs and interests of students who may live hundreds of miles apart. With online learning, students are now able to take foreign languages as diverse as German or Chinese, specialized science and math classes, advanced placement courses, and other kinds of instruction their traditional brick-and-mortar schools may not be able to provide. "Traditional schools are no longer limited by the teachers we can attract," Perry says. "I can offer Hebrew for one student, whereas in the old days, if I couldn't find a Hebrew teacher and 100 or more kids interested in Hebrew, we couldn't offer it."[47]

School districts that cannot afford to hire new teachers often *can* afford to offer students access to online classes, which allows those students to tap into a much wider variety of educational opportunities. Government programs and grants sometimes offset the expense of online classes and programs as well. Online schools are breaking down barriers created by geography and financial resources and providing students with diverse, high-quality educational choices.

Social Equity in the Classroom

Broad access to classes and subjects that may not be offered in one's neighborhood school is not the only advantage to online learning. Online schools also erase some of the social and cultural divisions that create conflict at school. Once students enroll in an online class, no one knows whether that student's home town is rural or urban, wealthy or struggling. For that matter, no one in an online class necessarily knows who among their peers might have a disability, or look different, or dress differently, or act differently from anyone else. Students instead are more likely to focus on what they have in common rather than differences. "Students who [attend] school online are not judged by fellow classmates according to their looks, their family's wealth, or other common denominators that sadly, many students in private and public schools are faced with,"[48] says one student at International Academy (iCademy, for short), a global virtual school provided by the online education software company K12 Inc.

Online school students report that they feel freer to speak up and contribute to class discussions, because they do not fear a room full of people who may seem judgmental. "I believe that online students, in general, are more expressive and open—they (students) give more of 'themselves' in an online environment,"[49] says Karen Bingham, an iCademy instructor. Online schools may have fewer (if any) bullies than brick-and-mortar schools. They simply can be places where students with similar interests gather to learn together.

An online class can include students from many different places, races, cultures, social backgrounds, and even age. The Internet allows them to hide differences about which they might feel self-conscious and share only the things about themselves they are comfortable sharing. For some online students, this results in greater self-confidence and feelings of acceptance among their school peers. In addition, online students potentially have even more opportunity than students at a neighborhood brick-and-mortar school to reap the benefits of socializing with people from diverse backgrounds and places.

Freedom to interact with people outside of the traditional school setting is a reason many students opt to try online learning in the first place. Adult students returning for a high school diploma or a college degree, for example, might feel uncomfortable about being older than the other students, but in a virtual classroom, age differences are unnoticeable. Online learning also appeals to students who want to attend school without leaving home. Students who live in outlying areas can have the benefits of a big-city school without leaving their family, lifestyle, and responsibilities. "Above all, online education is providing much greater freedom and flexibility for lifelong learning in that the very latest knowledge and information can be delivered and tailored to the needs and context of the learner, at a time when they need

it (just-in-time learning) to a place of their convenience,"[50] says computer science expert Mark Stansfield.

A Global Education

Online schools break geographic boundaries and also cultural ones. The Internet has revolutionized the way human beings communicate with each other. Social scientists refer to a shrinking world: people in different countries or on different continents, who once lived too far apart to associate easily with each other, are now able to interact online. The economy has become more global, too, meaning that companies and individuals around the world now buy and sell each other's products and services. Large businesses have become multinational, and the foundation of much commerce is information, rather than goods. Information travels through cyberspace rather than by rail or across the sea. Online schools give students the tools they need to navigate this shrinking and connected world.

Older adults may pursue an education online without having to commute to a learning center or feeling uncomfortable about not being as young as other students.

Saving Money with Online Schools

Technology in schools is costly. Computer labs, audiovisual equipment for teachers, online cataloguing systems for libraries, and other upgrades come at a hefty price. Online schools seem like yet another expensive technological upgrade. Yet, they are not nearly as pricey as some people assume. In fact, it costs less to educate a public K–12 student in an online school than it does to educate a student in a traditional brick-and-mortar school.

One source of the savings is the lack of physical buildings. Not having to build classrooms saves millions of dollars. Teaching staffs tend to be smaller, too. Online teachers are often able to handle larger class sizes than teachers who teach in traditional schools, meaning more students can attend with fewer teachers to conduct classes. Teacher salaries are often the largest ongoing expense in the school system, so paying fewer teachers saves a lot of money.

Online schools do have expenses, however. They ship boxes of books and school supplies to students and often send a computer as well. They also spend money developing websites, paying for students' Internet access, hiring course designers, and buying pre-made content for classes. Educating students online still costs money—the funds are just spent in different ways.

Traditional schools group students together by neighborhood when assigning them to a school and by age when assigning them to a class. Online schools give students opportunities to explore other places and cultures by assigning them to a class with anyone else who wants to take it. For the first time in history, students going to the same school can live in entirely different countries. Someone who wants to learn French or Chinese can even have a teacher and classmates who are native speakers living in France or

China. At the eTeacher Group's Online Language Academy, for example, students from anywhere in the world can take Chinese from a teacher who lives in Beijing or Hebrew from a teacher who lives in Israel. Online students have the potential to make connections and converse in real time with fellow students and teachers from almost anywhere.

By exposing students to peers with many different beliefs, cultures, lifestyles, and ideas, online education has the ability to be multicultural in a way that traditional brick-and-mortar classrooms, even with Internet connections that allow them to connect with other classes and people, have been much slower to accomplish. "The opportunities to socialize worldwide . . . [are] distinctly unique to the online learning environment," says Bingham. "The world has become smaller, and my students are tasting the flavors of other cultures. It becomes not a world 'all about me,' but a world 'all about us.' It's a beautiful thing!"[51]

Conserving the World

Just as students of online schools can immerse themselves in global cultures and learn to participate in a global economy, their choice to attend an online school also impacts the global environment. Traditional brick-and-mortar schools consume many resources. For example, the average American student in a traditional school throws away 320 lb (145kg) of paper each year. While online students use paper too, much of their work and their reading can be accomplished on the computer. They develop typing skills and use word-processing programs to turn in their papers, thus conserving trees and reducing paper waste.

Traditional schools use many resources besides paper. School buildings must be heated when the weather is cold and cooled on hot days, for example. Electricity is required to light every hallway, classroom, and gymnasium and to power educational tools like overhead projectors and the computers in a computer lab. Schools and their grounds also consume water to maintain playgrounds covered in grass or trees and bushes that are planted to make a campus look inviting.

Constructing, landscaping, maintaining, and powering a school building creates an extra source of energy consumption in a neighborhood. Online schools have fewer demands. Each student does use electricity in his or her home environment, but these same household resources might be in use anyway, especially if other family members are also home during the day.

The elimination of pollution that results from driving to and from school each day is another benefit of online schools. Fleets of buses are unnecessary when the commute to school is a trip from one room to another in the same house. Colorado's Provost Academy is an online school that prides itself on minimal impact to the environment. "With an online school there is no traffic, no gas being con-

Most traditional school districts require large fleets of school buses. A significant benefit of online schools is the amount of energy saved and pollution avoided when students are no longer required to get to and from school.

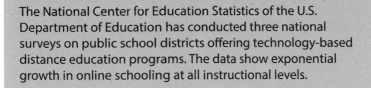

ONLINE LEARNING PROGRAMS IN U.S. PUBLIC SCHOOLS

The National Center for Education Statistics of the U.S. Department of Education has conducted three national surveys on public school districts offering technology-based distance education programs. The data show exponential growth in online schooling at all instructional levels.

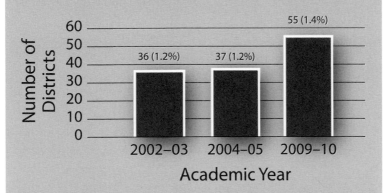

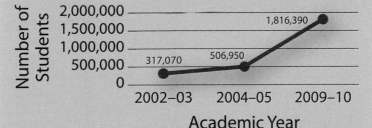

Data taken from: U.S. Department of Education, National Center for Education Statistics, Fast Response Survey System (FRSS), "Technology-Based Distance Education Courses for Public Elementary and Secondary Schools: 2002–03 and 2004–05," and "Distance Education Courses for Public Elementary and Secondary School Students: 2009–10." http://nces.ed.gov.

sumed by cars or buses to and from school," says Audie Rubin, the academy's executive director. "Further, there is less overall environmental impact since the school is not required to maintain classrooms which require lighting, heating and cooling, and maintenance." He also notes that the school and its students are careful about use of paper. "One of the only sheets of paper a student may receive from the Provost Academy may be the high school diploma they receive at the completion of their studies,"[52] Rubin says.

Economical Learning

Online schools are economical in other ways, too. Traditional teacher tasks such as taking attendance, grading daily quizzes, and calculating student grades can all be assumed

Becoming an Online Teacher

Job Description: Online teachers have many of the same responsibilities as traditional teachers—they just do the work online. They may record their lectures and also conduct synchronous (real-time) class sessions over the Internet. They assign, collect, and grade work and communicate with students by e-mail, online chatting, and phone. They also follow the policies of the school for which they work.

Education: Online teachers possess a bachelor's degree in education or their subject area. Most college instructors require a graduate degree.

Qualifications: Teachers in K–12 school settings require a teaching license in the state where they work. Online teachers may also require experience teaching in traditional classrooms and training or certification in online technology.

Additional Information: As more schools offer online courses, demand for online teachers is increasing. Many such instructors can work from a home office part or all of the time. They have often held traditional classroom teaching positions at a school before being chosen to teach its online classes.

Salary: About $50,000 a year for K–12 and $80,000 a year for college, comparable to the salaries of traditional classroom teachers.

by technology, freeing up teachers' time to focus on crafting lessons and helping individual students. As a result, teachers of online courses are able to enroll more students in each class, reducing the need for extra teaching staff. Online teachers can also reach far more students with a single lecture than is possible in a brick-and-mortar classroom—perhaps hundreds or even thousands of students at a time. "The best way to increase the quality of teaching is to increase the number of students taught by the best teachers," says college professor Alex Tabbarok. "Teaching students 30 at a time is expensive," he says. "Online education, however, dramatically increases the productivity of teaching . . . it's now possible for a single professor to teach more students in an afternoon than was previously possible in a lifetime."[53]

Recognizing the potential to reduce teachers' workload and educate students more efficiently, even traditional schools have begun to incorporate some aspects of online education into their programs, whether by recording their lectures to be viewed online or just by replacing redundant tasks like grading tests and reporting grades with computerized or online tools. Many schools also include online classes among their graduation requirements, so that their students reap some of the benefits of online learning. After all, online schools seem a natural fit in a world in which technology plays a leading role. Knowing how to navigate technology and exploit its powers are increasingly crucial, both in the job market and along the global information highway. Learning online marks an important milestone on that journey.

Online Schools for the Present and the Future

Students of online schools use the newest and latest computer and communication technology every day, preparing them for a working world that will expect them to do the same. Online education is no longer just a fad. Its many advantages make it an important part of the school experience. Hybrid schools—those that offer some in-person classes and some online courses during the school day—

are growing in popularity as traditional schools recognize the advantages of online learning. New technology and the Internet have put learning at people's fingertips, and the result has been an explosion in the number of students who like to take their classes in cyberspace.

Traditional school buildings are still the learning destination for the vast majority of students, especially in elementary and middle schools. However, even students at these levels are opting to learn online with increasing frequency. Colleges and universities face a growing demand for online classes, and in order to attract new students, they have responded with an increase in online course offerings. "Virtual schooling and online learning fit in extremely well with the emerging trend to embrace the same technologies that our young people are using in their everyday lives and apply them in education," says Catherine Cavanaugh, an associate professor at the University of Florida's College

Elementary school students in rural China crowd around a laptop during class. The Internet and computers have significantly altered education across the globe in both online and traditional schools.

of Education. "Schools that don't embrace online learning soon will be viewed as limiting the learning opportunities of their students."[54]

For now, traditional schools and teaching methods are in no danger of becoming obsolete. Someday, however, brick-and-mortar schools may be largely replaced by online alternatives. Not so long ago, it was hard to envision the prominent role that computers would play in learning. Now, it is even more difficult to imagine a school in which computers are absent.

NOTES

Introduction: School's Virtual Facelift

1. Bill Gates. "2010 Annual Letter from Bill Gates: Online Learning." 2010. www.gatesfoundation.org/annual-letter/2010/Pages/education-learning-online.aspx.

Chapter 1: A History of Learning Outside the Classroom

2. William H. Jeynes. *American Educational History: School, Society, and the Common Good*. Thousand Oaks, CA: Sage, 2007, p. 38.

3. Quoted in Kent Allen Farnsworth and Teresa Brawner Bevis. *A Fieldbook for Community College Online Instructors*. Washington, DC: American Association of Community Colleges, 2006, p. 6.

4. A.W. (Tony) Bates. *Technology, E-Learning, and Distance Education*, 2nd ed. New York: Routledge, 2005, p. 194.

5. Farnsworth and Bevis. *A Fieldbook for Community College Online Instructors*, p. 8.

6. Robert A. Wisher and Christina K. Curnow. "Video Based Instruction in Distance Learning: From Motion Pictures to the Internet." In *Handbook of Distance Education*, edited by Michael G. Moore and William Anderson. Mahwah, NJ: Lawrence Erlbaum Associates, 2003, p. 319.

7. Wisher and Curnow. "Video Based Instruction," p. 319.

8. Bernard Cohen. "Howard Aiken and the Dawn of the Computer Age." In *The First Computers: History and Architectures*, edited by Raúl Rojas and Ulf Hashagen. Cambridge, MA: MIT, 2002, p. 118.

9. Steve Ryan, Howard Freeman, Bernard Scott, and Daxa Patel. *The Virtual University: The Internet and Resource-Based Learning*. Sterling, VA: Stylus, 2000, p. 3.

10. Curtis J. Bonk. *The World Is Open: How Web Technology Is Revolutionizing Education*. San Francisco: Jossey-Bass, 2009, p. 92.

Chapter 2: The Technology of Online Education

11. Quoted in Kim Krisberg. "Online Public Health Education Grow-

ing in Popularity in U.S.: More Students Forgoing Classrooms." *The Nation's Health*, August 2012. http://thenationshealth.aphapublications.org/content/42/6/1.3.full.

12. Quoted in Steve Lohr. "Study Finds That Online Learning Beats the Classroom." *New York Times*, August 19, 2009. http://bits.blogs.nytimes.com/2009/08/19/study-finds-that-online-education-beats-the-classroom.

13. Quoted in David Nagel. "WiFi to Go: Middle Schoolers to Receive Mobile Hotspots." *The Journal*, August 10, 2010. http://thejournal.com/articles/2010/08/10/wifi-to-go-middle-schoolers-to-receive-mobile-hotspots.aspx.

14. Guy Klemens. *The Cellphone: The History and Technology of the Gadget That Changed the World*. Jefferson, NC: MacFarland and Company, 2010, p. 2.

15. Joseph Straubhaar, Robert LaRose, and Lucinda Davenport. *Media Now: Understanding Media, Culture, and Technology*, 7th ed. Boston, MA: Wadsworth, 2010, p. 358.

16. Straubhaar, LaRose, and Davenport. *Media Now*, p. 358.

17. Tim Berners-Lee. "Foreword." In *Spinning the Semantic Web: Bringing the World Wide Web to Its Full Potential*, edited by Dieter Fensel, James A. Hendler, Henry Lieberman, and Wolfgang Wahlster. Cambridge: Massachusetts Institute of Technology Press, 2005, p. xiii.

18. Romualdo Pastor-Satorras and Alessandro Vespignani. *Evolution and Structure of the Internet: A Statistical Physics Approach*. Cambridge, UK: Cambridge University Press, 2007, p. 12.

19. Pastor-Satorras and Vespignani. *Evolution and Structure of the Internet*, p. 1.

20. "Competition and the Internet." *Scientific American*, October 2010. www.scientificamerican.com/article.cfm?id=competition-and-the-internet.

21. Quoted in "Phone Service the Zero-Cost Way." *Bloomberg Businessweek*, January 5, 2004. www.businessweek.com/stories/2004-01-05/phone-service-the-zero-cost-way.

Chapter 3: Navigating an Online School

22. Quoted in Julie Sturgeon. "Creating an Effective Virtual School Program." *District Administration*, March 2007. www.districtadministration.com/article/creating-effective-virtual-school-program.

23. "Web Teacher Attendance." Administrative Software Applications. www.asacentral.com/attend2.html.

24. Stefan Hrastinski. "Asynchronous and Synchronous E-Learning." *Educause Quarterly*, October–December 2008. www.educause.edu/ero/article/asynchronous-and-synchronous-e-learning.

25. Hrastinski. "Asynchronous and Synchronous E-Learning."
26. Gerald W. Stone. *Core Macroeconomics*, 2nd ed. New York: Worth, 2012, p. xvi.
27. Eli Collins-Brown. "Multimedia in Online Courses: Bells and Whistles or Solutions?" Nineteenth Annual Conference on Distance Teaching and Learning. Madison, WI: University of Wisconsin, 2005. www.uwex.edu/disted/conference /Resource_library/proceedings/03 _59.pdf.
28. University of Central Florida Institute for Simulation and Training. "Just What Is 'Simulation' Anyway?" www.ist.ucf.edu/background.htm.
29. Kris Sloan. *Holding Schools Accountable: A Handbook for Educators and Parents*. Westport, CT: Praeger, 2007, p. 45.
30. Quoted in Kianti Roman. "Q&A: Libraries Turn New Page into Digital Age." *Yale News*, August 20, 2012. http://news.yale.edu/2012 /08/20/qa-libraries-turn-new -page-digital-age.
31. Quoted in Roman. "Q&A."
32. Kevin Ryan and James M. Cooper. *Those Who Can, Teach*, 13th ed. Belmont, CA: Wadsworth, 2012, p. 212.

Chapter 4: Drawbacks of Online Learning

33. Quoted in Steve Kolowich. "Score One for the Robo-Tutors." *Inside Higher Ed*, May 22, 2012. www.in sidehighered.com/news/2012/05 /22/report-robots-stack-human -professors-teaching-intro-stats.
34. Arne Duncan. "Finding Our True Center." *Homeroom*, July 1, 2011. www.ed.gov/blog/2011/07/finding -our-true-center.
35. Quoted in Amy McConnell Schaarsmith. "Growing Number of College Students Choose Online Courses." *Pittsburgh Post-Gazette*, February 16, 2012. www .post-gazette.com/stories/news /education/growing-number-of -college-students-choose-online -courses-85483/#ixzz25dgoXcjO.
36. Quoted in Stephanie Saul. "Profits and Questions in Online Charter Schools." *New York Times*, December 12, 2011. http://www.nytimes .com/2011/12/13/education/on line-schools-score-better-on-wall- street-than-in-classrooms.html.
37. Diane G. Smathers. *Phi Kappa Phi and the Distance Learner*. Baton Rouge, LA: Honor Society of Phi Kappa Phi, 2012. www.phi kappaphi.org/web/Publications /Distance_Ed_White_Paper.html.
38. Edward Lin. "'Virtual' Schools: Real Discrimination." *Seattle University Law Review*, vol. 32, no.1, 2008, p. 178.
39. Kevin Simpson. "Education's Digital Divide More About Bandwidth than Computer Hardware." *Denver Post*, August 20, 2012. www.denverpost.com/news/ci _21351636.
40. Mark Edmundson. "The Trouble

with Online Education." *New York Times*, July 19, 2012. www.nytimes .com/2012/07/20/opinion/the -trouble-with-online-education .html/.

41. David Elkind. "Playtime Is Over." *New York Times*, March 26, 2010. www.nytimes.com/2010/03/27 /opinion/27elkind.html?_r=1.

42. Elkind. "Playtime Is Over."

43. Katie R. Carone. "Online PE: Not Just a Virtual Workout." Southeast Education Network, March 31, 2010. www.seenmagazine.us/arti cles/article-detail/articleid/585/ online-pe.aspx.

Chapter 5: Advantages of Virtual Classrooms

44. John Palfrey and Urs Gasser. *Born Digital: Understanding the First Generation of Digital Natives*. New York: Basic Books, 2008, p. 2.

45. Steve Perry. "Are Virtual Schools Really an Answer?" *HLNtv*, April 30, 2012. www.hlntv.com/article /2012/04/26/virtual-schools-steve -perry-opinion.

46. Allan C. Ornstein, Daniel U. Levine, and Gerald L. Gutek. *Foundations of Education*, 11th ed. Belmont, CA: Wadsworth, 2011, p. 457.

47. Perry. "Are Virtual Schools Really an Answer?"

48. Quoted in Alexander Urpí. "The Socialization of Online School Students." *iCademy Globe*, January 21, 2010. www.icademyglobe .org/article.php?id=310.

49. Quoted in Urpí. "The Socialization of Online School Students."

50. Mark Stansfield. "Foreword." In *Online Education for Lifelong Learning*, edited by Yukiko Inoue. Hershey, PA: Information Science, 2007, p. viii.

51. Quoted in Urpí. "The Socialization of Online School Students."

52. Quoted in "Provost Academy— Colorado's Newest Eco-friendly High School." Provost Academy Colorado, August 2010. http:// co.provostacademy.com/news /press-release/provost-academy -colorados-newest-eco-friendly -high-school.

53. Alex Tabbarok. "Why Online Education Works." *Cato Unbound*, November 12, 2012. www.cato-un bound.org/2012/11/12/alex-tabar rok/why-online-education-works.

54. Quoted in "Online Classes Can Save Schools Money." *University of Florida News*, May 18, 2009. http://news.ufl.edu/2009/05/18 /online-learning.

GLOSSARY

analog: The process of taking an audio or video signal and translating it into electronic pulses sent as a continuous wave.

asynchronous learning: Learning that happens for different students at different places and times, or not occurring in "real time."

broadband: A method of high-speed Internet access that can send large amounts of data over lines or cables that do not compete with phone lines.

digital: Audio, video, or other data that has been broken down electronically into a two-digit format represented by a series of ones and zeroes.

Internet: A vast network connecting all computers worldwide and letting them communicate with shared computer language.

modem: A device that links a home computer to the Internet network.

packet: A small unit of data carried by a computer network such as the Internet.

protocol: A set of rules two computers use to connect to each other and share information.

router: A physical device that connects two computer networks within the Internet and directs data traffic traveling between senders and receivers.

synchronous learning: A group of people learning the same things at the same time, often in a shared location. Also known as "real time" instruction.

VoIP: Short for Voice over Internet Protocol, the method of transmitting voice and video communication over the Internet computer network.

WiFi: Short for wireless fidelity, networking technology that allows computers and other devices to communicate without wires.

World Wide Web: A set of electronic documents that make up a large part of the Internet, are written in hypertext language, and are searchable with Internet browser software.

Books

Andrew Blum. *Tubes: A Journey to the Center of the Internet*. New York: HarperCollins, 2012. This book explains the history of the Internet and how it has been built, structured, and connected so people throughout the world can use it to explore.

Lisa Lopuck. *Web Design for Dummies*, 3rd ed. Hoboken, NJ: John Wiley and Sons, 2012. This book explains the basics of how websites are built and how features are added, from graphics to interactive elements. It gives a designer's viewpoint of how websites, such as those of virtual schools, are constructed. Photographs, graphics, and cartoons make the book's content easier to understand.

Michele Sequeira and Michael Westphal. *Cell Phone Science: What Happens When You Call and Why*. Albuquerque, NM: University of New Mexico Press, 2011. This book takes readers on a tour of a cell phone's components, explains how phones use radio waves and cell towers to pass calls back and forth, and provides modern applications and etiquette for cell phone users.

Internet Sources

Caralee Adams. "Should All Schools Be Virtual?" *Scholastic*. www.scholastic.com/browse/article.jsp?id=3751959. This article discusses how virtual education differs from traditional classroom learning and what advantages are behind its growing popularity.

Amy Golod. "Educators Work to Better Integrate Technology into the Classroom." *U.S. News & World Report*, May 2, 2012. www.usnews.com/news/articles/2012/05/02/educators-work-to-better-integrate-technology-into-the-classroom. This article discusses different ways teachers are using technology and computers in online and traditional classrooms.

David Nagel. "Will Smart Phones Eliminate the Digital Divide?" *The Journal*, February 1, 2011. http://thejournal.com/articles/2011/02/01/will-smart-phones-eliminate-the-digital-divide.aspx. This article describes cell phones as the preferred technology of today's young generation and how the devices have the potential to end the digital divide standing between kids, teens, and online education.

Websites

iVirtual School: "How Do Virtual Schools Work?" (www.ivirtualsch ool.com/how-do-virtual-schools -work). This site discusses the various possibilities of virtual education, from online schools to programs that blend online and classroom learning. The site details what students can expect to see in modern online classrooms.

Online Schools E-book (www.online schools.org/e-book). This website, which is organized as a book with chapters, helps students decide whether online schooling may be right for them. Geared mainly toward students considering an online college, the site debunks common myths and explains the realities of getting an education online.

OnlineSchools.com (www.onlinesch ools.com). This site operated by online media company QuinStreet, Inc., explains how online schools work, from the elementary grades through graduate school. It addresses common questions and concerns and hints at what online school will be like in the future.

INDEX

A

Analog technology, 16, 30, 31
Animations, 45, 55, 56
Arizona State University, 36
ARPANET, 8, 24–25
Art courses, 26, 60
Asynchronous learning, 52–53, 68, *69*
Attendance records, 51, 67–68

B

Bell, Alexander Graham, 8, 17–18, *17*
Berkman Center for Internet and Society, 83
Berners-Lee, Tim, 9, 27, 41, *41*, 42, 70
Binary code, 239
Blackboard (software), 54
Blogs, 83
Broadband Internet access, 31, 40, 44, 46
Browsers, 42, *43*, 70, 84
Bullying, 76, 84, 85

C

Cable Internet connection, 31
California Virtual University, 9
Cell phone towers, *38*, 39
Cell phones, *8, 9,* 16, 37–39, *38*
Charter schools, 37
Cheating, 30, 71–72
Citizens band (CB) radio, 38–39
Class participation, 48, 54–56, 60–61, 68, 88
Class size, 30, 95

College education online
 correspondence courses, 20
 educational shortcut, 72–73
 famous graduates of online schools, 26
 flexibility and, *72,* 84–85, 88
 libraries, 63–64
 massive open online courses (MOOCs), 30
 online classes required, 11
 online college teachers, 94
 popularity, 10, 13, 82, 96
 rural students access, 15–16
 self-motivation and, 71
 University of Phoenix, 9, 28–29, *29*
 See also specific colleges and universities
College teachers, 94
Computer simulations, 57–59
Computers
 analog technology and, 30
 computer-based cameras, 48
 computing machines, 22–24
 education and, *11*
 e-mail, 25–26
 Ethernet cables, *35*
 laptops, *11, 32, 72, 96*
 modems, 36
 networking, 24–26
 radio signals and, 36
 servers, 51–52, *51*
 tablets, 32, 40, *56*, 60
 wireless connections and, 31–32, 36, 44–45, *44*
 See also Internet; Technology; World Wide Web

cell phones, *8, 9*, 16, *38*
cell phones and online learning, 37–39
computers and, 24
development, *8, 9*, 17–18, *17*
digital technology, 16
Internet compared with telephone system, 34
invention of, *8, 8*
Television, 21–22, *21,* 24
Tests and quizzes, 61, 71–72
Texting, 76

U

UCLA (University of California, Los Angeles), 8, 24
United States Distance Learning Association, 50
Universal resource locator (URL), 41, 70
University of Central Florida's Institute for Simulation and Training, 59
University of Chicago, 15
University of Houston, 8
University of Phoenix, 9, 28–29, *29*
U.S. Centers for Disease Control (CDC), 78
U.S. Department of Education, 62, 68, 84, *93*
U.S. Postal Service, 15

V

Video conferencing, *61*

Video games, 25, 43, 55–56, 66, 68, 77, 78
Virtual flashcards, 56
Virtual science labs, 57–59
Voice over Internet Protocol (VoIP)
    diagram of workings, *47*
    international classrooms and, *49*
    Skype and, 48
    synchronous classrooms and, 54
    verbal communication over Internet, 46, 48–49

W

Washington Internet Academy, 9
Water conservation, 92
Web browsers, 42, *43*, 70, 84
Webinars, 53
WiFi, 9, *9*, 36–37, 39–40
Windle, Jordan, 26
Wireless connections
    online schools, 31–32, *32*
    routers and, *35,* 36, 44–45, *44*
Wireless telegraph, 18
World Wide Web
    browsers, 42, *43*, 70, 84
    development, 27–28, 41, 70
    Hypertext markup language (HTML) and, 41–43
    websites, 43–44
    See also Internet; Technology

PICTURE CREDITS

Jenny MacKay has written twenty nonfiction books for kids and teens on topics such as crime scene investigation, sports science, and technology. Her son and daughter attend an online elementary school and access all of their classes from laptop computers with wireless Internet connections.